THE VIGIL

26 DAYS IN CRAWFORD, TEXAS

Eyewitness to History as
Seen Through the Eyes
of Grass-Roots Reporters

W. LEON SMITH
Publisher of *The Lone Star Iconoclast*

Featuring Reports, Interviews & Perspectives by
Nathan Diebenow
Deborah Mathews
Gene Ellis Sills, Ed.D.
Michael Harvey

DS
.4

© 2005 Smith Media, Inc.

Cover image: © Jason Reed/Reuters/Corbis
Cover design: Ralph Bernardo
Text design & layout: Maya Shmuter
Editor: Liz Lawler

Published by The Disinformation Company Ltd.
163 Third Avenue, Suite 108
New York, NY 10003
Tel.: +1.212.691.1605
Fax: +1.212.691.1606
www.disinfo.com

Library of Congress Control Number: 2005936576

ISBN-13: 978-1-932857-33-7
ISBN-10: 1-932857-33-8

Printed in USA

10 9 8 7 6 5 4 3 2 1

Distributed in the USA and Canada by:
Consortium Book Sales and Distribution
1045 Westgate Drive, Suite 90
St Paul, MN 55114
Toll Free: +1.800.283.3572 Local: +1.651.221.9035
Fax: +1.651.221.0124
www.cbsd.com

Distributed in the United Kingdom and Eire by:
Virgin Books
Thames Wharf Studios, Rainville Road
London W6 9HA
Tel.: +44.(0)20.7386.3300 Fax: Tel.: +44.(0)20.7386.3360
E-Mail: sales@virgin-books.co.uk

Distributed in Australia by:
Tower Books
Unit 2/17 Rodborough Road
Frenchs Forest NSW 2086
Tel.: +61.2.9975.5566 Fax: +61.2.9975.5599
Email: towerbks@zip.com.au

*For all the freedom-fighters, champions of
the U.S. Constitution, and most of all, Iconoclasts
over time who have deposited upon our spirits
the values of truth and hope.*

CONTENTS

THE VIGIL 26 DAYS IN CRAWFORD, TEXAS

FOREWORD
Cindy Sheehan

The first time I heard of *The Lone Star Iconoclast* was when the paper courageously endorsed John Kerry for President in 2004. I was so impressed with the paper, and with the progressive community's response to it. When all the advertisers withdrew their ads, progressives across the nation pitched in and bought enough subscriptions to keep the paper going. Even in my despair at losing Casey, and even with the disappointment (despite *The Iconoclast*'s endorsement) of Bush's victory in 2004, I knew that this was a paper to be respected.

But I never thought at that time that I would become such an integral part of their August 2005 reporting, or that the staff of the paper would become so familiar to me.

The media attention I received in Crawford was overwhelming, and often disheartening. I had been trying for months to break into the mainstream media to highlight the abuses of the Bush administration and to underscore the fact that the mainstream media has worked to keep Iraq out of the sight and minds of middle Americans.

I saw the media supporting the insane build-up to war by not asking the President and his war council the tough questions they should have, such as: "Why are you saying that Iraq has weapons of mass destruction when the UN weapons inspectors say otherwise?" or "Why are you linking Saddam with 9/11?" And, most importantly: "Why are you heading pell-mell towards disaster and sending our brave troops to fight, die, and kill in a country that doesn't appear to be any threat to our national security?" These questions and others could have been asked... and asked... and asked until they were answered satisfactorily.

Whatever happened to investigative reporting?

The media heralded the "shock and awe" campaign in March 2003, but the huge protests worldwide against the war in February 2003 barely registered on either George Bush or the media's radar. The media also didn't report on the killing of so many civilian lives as a result of the "shock and awe" campaign and the subsequent invasion. The media have gone along with the War Department's policy of not counting the corpses they call "collateral damage"; they have also failed to report on the widespread torture tactics of the U.S. military, except to focus on the pictures of seemingly normal Americans committing abnormal atrocities on fellow human beings. The Abu Ghraib torture scandal that Seymour Hersch, a true investigative journalist and courageous reporter, exposed in May 2004 should have blown this scandalous war apart, but the media, who seem to be complicit with the government's war crimes, buried the story with the other victims.

There have been so many events in the history of this invasion and occupation that should have been hammered on by the media—but, instead, they regularly get their feather dusters out and give Bush a light touch before going on to the next celebrity scandal. Yet I remember that George Bush lied about "yellow cake" uranium in the 2003 State of the Union address, that Valerie Plame was subsequently outed, and that Bush declared "an end to major combat" in Iraq on May 1, 2003. I recall the capture of Saddam Hussein, and the findings of the 9/11 Commission report, which were followed by the Senate Intelligence report, the Duelfer "no WMDs" report, the Downing Street memos… shall I continue, or are we getting the picture?

In September 2004, our 1,000th soldier was killed in Iraq. The news that week was all about Scott Peterson. The media showed hundreds of people in front of the courthouse waving their signs and screaming with bloodthirsty joy when he was found guilty. I thought to myself then: "When is the public going to come out in these numbers to protest the war?" and "When will the families of the 1,000 soldiers that this callous excuse for an administration sent to die in an immoral war see justice? When will the people of Iraq finally be able to live in peace?"

In January 2005, I was slated to go on *Larry King Live* after the elections in Iraq. I was going to be asked if I thought Casey's sacrifice was "worth it." I thought that was a fair question and I was prepared to ask Larry if he would have one of his children killed on the altar of greed in exchange for a sham election. All of the preparation went for naught, though, because I was bumped—the Michael Jackson molestation trial started that day.

I went to Crawford, Texas on August 6, 2005 to ask George Bush one simple question: "What noble cause did my son die for?" I didn't even realize the mainstream media would be there in force (and very bored). I should have seen where things were going, though, when I was on Wolf Blitzer's show the first morning after I sat in the ditch. His producer in Crawford told me: "You planned this perfectly, there's nothing going on." I said: "Oh really, there's nothing going on? Twenty-four soldiers and Marines were killed in Iraq this week. Tell their families there's nothing going on." She replied, "Well, you know what I mean." No, I didn't know what she meant. Iraq should be on the front page of every paper and the lead story of every news program, whether there is a mom sitting in a ditch in Crawford or not. The media have gone along with the government in sanitizing this. They agree with Barbara Bush, who said on ABC's *Good Morning America* on March 18, 2003, that she didn't want her "beautiful mind" cluttered with such things as returning caskets.

Another irony of the Crawford situation was the way that the media joyfully and spitefully scrutinized everything I have ever written, said, or done. I am just a mom from California trying to end a war before any other moms get their hearts and souls ripped out. George Bush is responsible for serial killing on an enormous scale, and he has yet to be called to task for saying that Saddam had weapons of mass destruction that could reach the east coast in forty-five minutes. I also found it highly ironic that most of the media privately supported me, but publicly castigated or ridiculed me.

I believe the media are partly responsible for the invasion and our continued presence in Iraq. They still won't ask the hard questions, particularly: "What noble cause?" I also believe that everyone in America has blood on their hands for this monstrosity, some of us more than others. If the media did their job, we never would have invaded Iraq. And if they would do their job now, we would be getting out of there soon.

The hurricanes and recent bird flu hype have again eclipsed Iraq. The media is delighted to distract our country from the ongoing war crimes in Iraq—but some publications shine the spotlight directly where it belongs, and *The Lone Star Iconoclast* is one such publication. Publishing this material in such a hostile environment is especially commendable. It gives me hope that there is some integrity in the media, and that this paper could be a beacon for other media outlets.

The Iconoclast's reporting from Camp Casey was always balanced and fair. The one day when the "anti-Sheehan" crowd came, *The Iconoclast* interviewed many people from the other side.

In the end, we only want fairness in reporting. The mainstream media's slant has been largely pro-war and the pro-peace view rarely gets an audience with middle America. I guess I should be glad that the reporters and other media personalities were "bored" that August. In a rare instance (but for the wrong reasons), the media did a good thing. We had thousands of Americans come to support Camp Casey, and millions who couldn't come kept up with our activities through the media and especially *The Iconoclast*, which blogged almost constantly from our peace camp.

In August 2005, from a ditch outside Crawford, we demanded accountability of George Bush. I think it's time we forced the media to adhere to the high ethical standards of W. Leon Smith, publisher of *The Iconoclast,* which shine like a lone spark of integrity in the prairie darkness.

I hope you enjoy this book as much as I enjoyed getting to know the staff at *The Iconoclast*. I know it will give you a very important perspective on why Camp Casey captured so many hearts and imaginations.

INTRODUCTION

While Cindy Sheehan and her legion of supporters awaited an audience with President Bush from her encampment in a ditch near the Central Texas community of Crawford, *The Lone Star Iconoclast* and its staff members began a vigil of their own. The publisher of the weekly newspaper, without notice or preparation, decided to utilize the newspaper's online edition to provide frequent updates from reporters in the field in addition to their regular reports, an action that stretched virtually all the newspaper's resources to the limit for twenty-six tempestuous days in August 2005.

The vigil began on Saturday, August 6, 2005, as Cindy Sheehan reacted boldly to statements made by President Bush regarding "the noble cause" for which our troops have fought in Iraq. Sheehan's initiative in Crawford ended twenty-six days later, after thousands of individuals had braved scorching Texas temperatures during the hottest days of the summer season to take part in history.

Sheehan, the mother of a soldier killed in Iraq, had with great emotion taken exception to the President's use of dead soldiers as a reason to continue the war. She wanted to speak to the President, face-to-face, to question his reasons for continuing the war and his ever-changing reasons for starting the war. The "War President" had embarked on his annual extended vacation from the worries of the presidency and, it had been announced, would be at the ranch, off and on, for about five weeks. Sheehan was determined to camp near his Prairie Chapel ranch in the boondocks near Crawford until he came out to speak with her.

Several anti-war groups accompanied Sheehan on her impromptu journey to Crawford, to provide support and to raise a multitude of objections to America's involvement in the war.

The Lone Star Iconoclast was there at the very beginning, at the end, and most of the time in between. This story traces many of the events as they unfolded, and provides insight as to how the newspaper provided coverage from the grass-roots level.

Upon Sheehan's arrival in Crawford, *The Iconoclast* launched a segment on its website called "Cindy Watch," which was not necessarily written in typical newspaper style.

There were parts of it that did adhere to that style. However, the publisher attempted to attain a more immediate, on-the-spot feel for most of it, somewhat reminiscent of the style utilized in Herbert Morrison's eyewitness report of the 1937 Hindenburg disaster from the landing field where he exclaimed, "Oh, the humanity!" as the burning dirigible was poised to crash.

The journalists were eyewitnesses who dictated their reports to the publisher who sat at his computer eighteen miles away.

Interspersed into the chapters that follow are most of these on-the-spot accounts, commentary about the discussions and obstacles the newspaper encountered along the way, and a few of the notable interviews and news accounts that rounded out the coverage.

At the conclusion of the day-by-day segments, commentaries by some of the reporters who braved the heat and risked life and limb at the rallies are published.

DAY ONE
Saturday, August 6, 2005

In addition to various editorials, this book includes text compiled and written from oral reports as dictated by Lone Star Iconoclast *journalists in the field.*

The planned cover story for the Vol. 6, No. 32 edition of *The Lone Star Iconoclast* was not about Cindy Sheehan. It was about the organization known as Teaching Peace in Texas.

A Friday convention in Arlington, Texas sponsored by Texans for Peace was being covered by staff writer Nathan Diebenow. He was also in line to cover the visit of Dr. Satoru Konishi, a Hiroshima survivor, who was a guest speaker there.

Earlier in the week, on Wednesday, Diebenow had received an advisory by e-mail mentioning that Cindy Sheehan would be journeying to Crawford for her fateful non-meeting with President Bush.

Sheehan said that, out of the blue, she had made the decision to stay, if necessary, an entire month outside the Bush ranch, seeking to talk to the President in person.

Diebenow phoned Sheehan that night for more information, and had come away with the idea that perhaps this should be covered on Saturday instead of the Texans for Peace convention.

As publisher, I was torn between the two stories, since Sheehan's initiative could carry considerable emotion but appeared to have flimsy planning, while the other story had been carefully planned and was a sure bet for "Iconoclastic treatment."

It was a tough call.

Tentatively, we decided to stick with the Texans for Peace story, as our normal deadline was "now" and we were running behind schedule. To change course would mean, for me, another sleepless Sunday night. I didn't want to come up empty-handed at the eleventh hour with no main story after chasing a vanishing rabbit.

On Saturday morning, we were clicking toward deadline at the proper cadence, save for the phone ringing off the hook with readers wondering whether the Sheehan story would be covered.

More e-mails than normal were coming across the internet, many politely demanding that Sheehan not be ignored.

One phone-caller asked if *The Iconoclast* would be posting updates about Sheehan during the day, since there were people all over the country interested in this story.

Finally, I called Diebenow, who was in the Metroplex and we talked it out. Sheehan or the convention?

Since Konishi was scheduled to also speak at the Crawford Peace House just prior to Sheehan's arrival, we decided that the Crawford story might carry more weight after all. We could get both the Hiroshima story and the Sheehan story from that locale.

This, of course, would mean pushing to the hilt our 4 a.m. final deadline on Monday to have the print edition at the printing plant.

To make deadline matters worse, we decided to follow the advice of the caller who suggested we post immediate updates on the website. Here, we would be experimenting in a strange new world—a weekly newspaper suddenly going live, or thereabouts.

There had been absolutely no preparations made in advance for this, and to add to the difficulty, our website was not laid out for this type of abuse.

Diebenow came to Clifton for last minute strategizing on how the coverage would transpire, then went to Crawford to cover Konishi and remain for Sheehan's arrival by bus. We would play the rest by ear.

Later that morning, I posted this on the website www.icono-clast-texas.com:

The Lone Star Iconoclast is covering Saturday's journey to Crawford by several groups, including Veterans for Peace, Military Families Speak Out, Iraq Veterans Against The War, CodePink, Crawford Peace House, and others.

Cindy Sheehan, the mother of a soldier killed in Iraq last year, is seeking a meeting with President Bush, who is vacationing in Crawford, to have some of her questions answered about the war. Several busloads of interested individuals are expected in Crawford to support her cause. Sheehan has said that she is willing to camp out in Crawford until she gets to meet with the President.

Iconoclast reporter Nathan Diebenow is on the scene and will be dispatching reports during the day. As they come in they will be reported here.

11:30 a.m. Nathan Diebenow reporting:

Konishi said he wants the government of Japan to give money to the Japanese victims of the bombing because for a long time the Japanese government did not acknowledge that the radiation had an effect on the people of the areas of Nagasaki and Hiroshima. He expressed no ill will toward the people of the United States. He said he wants the ban of all nuclear weapons.

12:40 p.m. Nathan Diebenow reporting:
SHEEHAN'S ARRIVAL BY BUS.

Following the bus is a train of automobiles, numbering over fifteen.

Sheehan said she is prepared to go to jail if necessary, but is expecting a peaceful confrontation.

[First issue of *The Iconoclast* devoted to Cindy Sheehan's activities.]

Currently, a bus provided by Veterans for Peace is taking about a dozen members, including Cindy Sheehan, to the checkpoint in front of President Bush's ranch. Sheriff's Department Captain Kenneth Vanek said prior to departing to lead the caravan, "As long as y'all work with us, we'll work with y'all."

Thus began the reports that would ultimately lead to that edition's headline: "President Bush Ditches Mother of Slain Soldier."

1:10 p.m. Nathan Diebenow reporting:

We've got about fifty-something people walking on the side of the road, in a ditch, all the way up the mile to the Bush ranch. At the first checkpoint, the police ordered them to not walk on the roadway, but in the medium-tall grass along the right side of the road where it is about ten feet wide in places, three feet deep in some places. They are kind of straddling the roadway.

There appears to be another checkpoint up ahead, with another car in the middle of the road.

Now two big white dogs are coming out to greet them along the fence. I don't know what kind of dogs they are, but they seem to be friendly. Some rancher's probably.

It's really hot, humid, with people sweating.

Wait. Call you back in a minute.

1:15 p.m. Nathan Diebenow reporting:

We are at the second checkpoint and the Sheriff's Department has told the protestors to get off the road. They've been walking on the road, breaking their part of the bargain, the police say.

Some in Cindy's group are now sitting, waiting for Bush to come out. Now more are sitting down.

One Veterans for Peace protestor asked police officers

for water because it's a hundred degrees.

Now the protestors are reciting the Lord's Prayer in unison.

(Moments later)—now Cindy Sheehan is shouting that Bush's mother ought to be ashamed of him. She's proud of her child who died in Iraq.

I now see Secret Service out here.

Protestors are saying that one of their rationales for not getting off the road was that the media was on the road. A police officer said that the media was just following the protestors, but the media is still on the road, with cameras, booms, microphones.

Some protestors are still sitting, but more are now standing.

They are now chanting "No Justice, No Peace." "George Bush is a war criminal." "Downing Street memos prove it." "Billion dollars a week for war."

Chanting again, people on the left saying, "Had enough," people on the right saying "Stop the war." They're going back and forth.

Police are now telling the media to get on the other side of the road and to not disrupt traffic.

Chanting is still going on (time 1:20 p.m.).

More coming.

2:10 p.m. Nathan Diebenow reporting:

At the first checkpoint, Sheehan told Officer Vanek: "We don't have the quarrel with you. The quarrel we have is with the President."

At the second checkpoint, she said: "I didn't come all the way from California to stand here in a ditch."

An officer offered to send Bush a letter or a statement from Cindy Sheehan, but she said she didn't want to do that.

Her reply was that they were making the mother of a

veteran of the Iraq war walk in a ditch.

Protestors are carrying signs that read "No more blood for oil," "Support our troops, bring them home now," and "Frodo failed. Bush has the ring."

It is extremely hot. People are starting to get dehydrated.

Sheehan is moving toward the ranch at the second checkpoint and says, "In the name of 1,828 soldiers that should be alive, I'm going to go see the President. He killed my son."

An officer got in her face, stopping her.

The crowd starts chanting, "W. killed her son. W. killed her son."

Bush has not come out, none of those anti-protest protestors either.

Hadi Jawad, a board member of the Crawford Peace House, shouts to the media: "Do your job. Ask about the Downing Street memo."

After sitting in the heat waiting to interview Cindy, most members of the press start to leave. Now protestors start to leave. One says, "I guess we ought to go." It appears that the initial protest is over.

Sheehan says she is going to stay at the checkpoint. Others are bringing water to her. The idea seems to be that she intends to camp out here, but I am unsure at this point whether the authorities will allow it. The others are going back to the Peace House to regroup.

Cindy Sheehan said after the media had left: "This is the beginning of the end of the occupation of Iraq." A wild round of applause followed.

Currently, the Secret Service and the police are just hanging around. The area is beginning to look deserted except for Cindy and her small group.

3:10 p.m. Nathan Diebenow reporting:

The police are giving Cindy a hard time because they

won't let her set up a tent by the side of the road.

This will probably be the last dispatch for awhile.

People became ill after walking the ditches.

Dehydration was rampant. Emotions ran high.

Our reporter, after returning to the office, downloaded photographs and wrote captions, then called it a day. He had missed lunch during the marathon rally and was sporting a sunburn. It had been a highly charged, stressful day that could have erupted into another Kent State.

I attempted several times to call Cindy Sheehan to learn the latest. She had been at the Peace House, recuperating, herself quite ill.

Finally, around 7 p.m., she acquiesced to a short conversation.

I filed the online report at 7:15 p.m.:

Iconoclast publisher W. Leon Smith visited with Cindy Sheehan just a few minutes ago. She was cooling off at the Peace House in Crawford.

Sheehan said she intends to continue to attempt to gain an audience with President Bush and will go back to the checkpoint tonight, where she will camp beside the road.

Sheehan commented that a brainstorm of an idea she had Wednesday has snowballed into this, with support from all over the country.

"I'm filled with hope now, too, that we might be able to turn things around," she said.

Earlier in the afternoon, after most of the individuals departed the second checkpoint, Sheehan says she was greeted with representatives from the Western White House who offered to take a message to President Bush. She says she told them her concerns, but that she was there to speak directly to the President.

In a message through *The Iconoclast* to the President

she said, "George Bush, if you really care about me, why aren't you meeting with me?"

Sheehan noted that additional support is on its way from throughout the country as she continues her efforts, which will include a candlelight vigil. Caravans from Louisiana and San Diego are on the way, to name a couple, she said.

DAY TWO
Sunday, August 7, 2005

The second day of Cindy Sheehan's mission to speak with the President was somewhat quiet, as she and her supporters recuperated from Saturday's walk in the ditch. Since there were no open demonstrations and the newspaper was deep into recording the prior day's events for the print edition, we chose to offer a summary report online, along with photos we took, while plans for the coming week were being discussed.

Summary report:
During the day Sunday, Sheehan received numerous votes of thanks, well-wishes, and support from around the globe, said Diane Wilson, founding member of CodePink, a national anti-war group. While Sheehan was doing interviews Sunday afternoon, small groups of supporters were arriving at her campsite, dropping off supplies and enjoying the cloudy weather on Prairie Chapel Road.

Wilson announced Sunday that she is starting a hunger strike in Crawford aimed at getting President Bush to talk with Cindy Sheehan, mother of a U.S. soldier slain in

Iraq. According to CodePink's website Sunday evening, three others have joined the strike: Jodie Evans, Cindy Sheehan's sister DeDe Miller, and Sarah Rath. Wilson said she believes that more volunteers will follow suit around the country in the coming days.

Friends of Peace and Justice of Waco are in the process of mobilizing support for Sheehan's month-long vigil.

DAY THREE
Monday, August 8, 2005

The Iconoclast brought in another reporter on Monday, as battle over turf began for Cindy Sheehan and her newly-named "Camp Casey."

Nathan Diebenow had in previous weeks split his time between duties with *The Iconoclast* and the neighboring *Clifton Record* newspapers, but had recently opted to cease his duties with *The Record* to spend time at creative writing endeavors.

He had remained employed part-time, however, writing and doing investigations for *The Iconoclast*.

His replacement at *The Record* was Deborah Mathews, whose main duties had been related to the Clifton newspaper. Since Diebenow departed on Monday to pursue other story obligations, Mathews was asked to begin reporting for *The Iconoclast* with updates, her first real assignment for the Crawford newspaper.

Mathews recalled her debut at *The Iconoclast*:

"How do you feel about being arrested?" was my introduction to the Cindy Sheehan story.

My editor-in-chief asked this of me in a calm, steady voice and simply waited for my reply.

My reply was: "Not great, how about you?"

After a ridiculously long wait, Leon explained to me about Cindy Sheehan's visit to Crawford and that he wanted me to help cover her visit.

Two sentences into the explanation, I knew that being involved with this in any way would be something I would be uncomfortable with, but… the experience would be one of a kind. As hard as I tried to talk myself out of agreeing to report on Cindy Sheehan and her cause, I could not.

My initial impression of Camp Casey was: "What's all the fuss about?" A few tents were staked out and several haphazard-looking signs were strewn here and there—not much to get excited about. To intensify my already growing irritation, I had taken the wrong road, twice, trying to find the place!

My instructions had been to go out, try to meet with Cindy, get a general feeling for how things were progressing and report back.

Well, Cindy wasn't there, progression wasn't apparent, and I was prepared to report that this was ridiculous.

Determined to do a thorough job, I drove to the Crawford Peace House. Nothing impressive there either—signs, and a woman lying on the floor and talking on a cell phone.

She smiled and said, "Can I help you?"

As politely as I could, I told her that I was trying to find someone who could talk with me about this Cindy Sheehan and what she was doing here.

The woman replied, "I'm Cindy. I'll talk with you as soon as I finish this interview."

I did get to talk with her and nothing could have prepared me for that woman. I'm not sure what I expected, but Cindy Sheehan was soft spoken and sincerely kind. She seemed so gentle, just as she seemed so determined.

Word came that the camp would be removed by the Sheriff's Department and Cindy and I began that day's interview at sixty-five miles-per-hour, headed from the Peace House to Camp Casey, with questions thrown in between incoming calls from supporters and her calls to her lawyer.

Being with her during the first days of her journey, I could have never predicted that the woman in my car would become what she became. The experience was one of a kind.

Here is Deborah Mathews' interview with Cindy Sheehan, as Mathews drove Sheehan to Camp Casey. Said Mathews: "Cindy Sheehan was in my car when the Sheriff was arriving to post 'no trespassing' signs..."

ICONOCLAST: I want to know how you got the information that there would be arrests made on Thursday?
SHEEHAN: A Texas legislator called our camp today to tell us.
ICONOCLAST: What they did say, in fact, was that there would be arrests made because you were a threat to —
SHEEHAN: If we didn't leave.
ICONOCLAST: As a threat to national security, that's what they said?
SHEEHAN: As a threat to the President of the United States.
ICONOCLAST: Threatening how? And why are you a threat to him on Thursday and not today?
SHEEHAN: Exactly. I don't know.

Sheehan left a voice message for her attorney, David. She continued to call the situation an emergency as she hung up with people on incoming calls.

SHEEHAN: I have got to calm down because I can't act like a crazy lady.

ICONOCLAST: Have you got family here with you?

SHEEHAN: Not right now. These people here are all my family. Let me try to get in touch with my other attorney. I left a message with another attorney, Jeff Harrington. He's the lawyer that defended some other people that got arrested.

ICONOCLAST: That did, in fact, happen.

SHEEHAN: Yeah.

ICONOCLAST: What were they arrested for?

SHEEHAN: Trespassing.

ICONOCLAST: Has the Secret Service interacted with you at all?

SHEEHAN: Yeah. Saturday. They said that if we stayed here we would probably get hit by a car. *(Pause, while dialing.)* I can't get a hold of anybody.

ICONOCLAST: Let your people know that they need to get in touch with us, as it develops. We did get an e-mail from someone who talked about a complete difference in your opinion from the first time you met Bush —

SHEEHAN: That's not true.

ICONOCLAST: Okay. Let me hand it to you *(the e-mail)*. I wanted you to see that and I would like to print your response to that.

SHEEHAN: I've already heard about this and I've talked about it, but...

ICONOCLAST: You made a comment earlier with one of the other reporters about being in shock at that time and I believe this is what you were discussing—that you were in shock and you're not in shock anymore.

SHEEHAN: Right. I'm not in shock anymore. So many reports have come out—the Senate Intelligence report, the 9/11 Commission report, the Downing Street memos—that show that my son's murder was premeditated and unnecessary and I'm still a grieving mother, but I'm not in shock anymore.

I am just very angry that my son is in a grave and for no reason. My son and almost 1,900 other brave Americans and tens of thousands of innocent Iraqis are dead for lies and that infuriates me and nobody is being held account-able for that. So, it's okay for the right-wing talk show hosts to scrutinize everything a grieving mother in shock says, but they won't scrutinize something the President says that caused the senseless death of so many people. To me, that's an obscenity.

ICONOCLAST: I understand.

SHEEHAN: That's about it, you know.

ICONOCLAST: Tell me what it was that prompted you to do this. Obviously, you want to deal with the President face-to-face, is that correct?

SHEEHAN: Yeah. Well, you know, I never really thought that was possible when I came out and I think it's less than possible now. My real goal is to put the war back on the front pages where it belongs. If people in America don't know that we actually have a war going on, how are they going to organize to stop it? The media—their attention is so focused on other things—Terri Schiavo and Michael Jackson and that unfortunate family whose daughter is missing in Aruba, which is tragic, but not as tragic as tens of thousands of people being dead for nothing. All I've wanted to do since Casey died is to put a human face on this war and to stop the suffering.

Phone call interrupts: Diane Wilson explains to Sheehan that the Sheriff said that they can only stay where the banners are.

SHEEHAN: We can only stay at the place where the banners are.

ICONOCLAST: Why?

SHEEHAN: They said that all the property is hers—even the road.

ICONOCLAST: Who said that?

SHEEHAN: The lady that owns the property.

ICONOCLAST: When I spoke with one of your representatives this morning, she said that someone had apparently gotten upset because some banners had blown onto or were moved onto her land. As it turned out, that was not her land. Did you have to move any at that time?

SHEEHAN: We did. We have all the banners in the place where we can keep the banners now.

ICONOCLAST: So there is no more dispute about that?

SHEEHAN: Right, but the cars—we can't leave the cars there. Anything that's on that land will be confiscated.

ICONOCLAST: Did she say if the Sheriff is still out there?

SHEEHAN: I believe he still is.

ICONOCLAST: I'm a little bit surprised that it's the Sheriff and not Secret Service.

SHEEHAN: Well, it can't be Secret Service. Why would you be surprised?

ICONOCLAST: I expect just to see them out overseeing all of this.

SHEEHAN: Well, they are. You know that's why they're out here.

Phone call interrupts again. Sheehan sets up a 5:30 interview.

ICONOCLAST: Before I let you go, is there anything that you want said, that you haven't said a thousand times already, on this website?

SHEEHAN: I don't think so.

She seems really stressed.

ICONOCLAST: Are you all right?

SHEEHAN: Yeah.

ICONOCLAST: Do you want to get out or do you want to —

SHEEHAN: Yeah. I want to get out.

Mathews' first report came in at 12:05 p.m. Monday:

Cindy Sheehan spent the night in her tent beside the road last night and has spent the morning on the telephone in the Peace House being interviewed by the media. Right now she is there alone.

She seems to be doing well, but looks tired.

License plates from other states are seen throughout downtown Crawford as business appears to be booming. The Coffee Station is crowded.

4:55 p.m. Deborah Mathews reporting:

It's really wild.

Someone from the Sheriff's Department is out here right now. He gave the campers twelve minutes to move their vehicles from the triangular piece of turf near the road. Otherwise, the "vehicles will be under arrest," he said. They will be towed.

Cindy rode back to camp with me. She said she was told by a legislator that if she is still here on Thursday that she will be arrested because she is a "threat to the President."

She said that newspapers and media are not covering the war in Iraq. Her goal here is to bring attention back to the fact that tens of thousands of people are being killed.

Right now this minute, the Sheriff's Department officer is here. He says the campers have eight more minutes to vacate their vehicles. He said: "If I have to call a tow truck, I will."

Cindy's cell phone has been ringing non-stop. She hangs up and it immediately rings.

Some of the campers are asking why the officers didn't know previously that the vehicles couldn't be parked by the road in that area.

One camper said of the order to vacate: "Now that's convenient!"

Cindy said: "Fine, let's move the vehicles and we'll just run people back and forth out there."

There's a county commissioner out here, too. I'll get his name later.

Now there's a law enforcement car flying ninety-to-nothing out there.

It's now sprinkling, with some thunder, very gray. Someone said the storm had a lot of red in it, "We don't want her on a cell phone out there." My car thermometer reads seventy-nine degrees.

5:14 p.m. Deborah Mathews reporting:

The name of the Sheriff's deputy is Sergeant John Kolinek and the County Commissioner is Ray Meadows.

People were forced to not only move the vehicles, but also the tents off that triangular piece of ground, which is apparently owned by some woman. Law enforcement says that this action is based on "prescriptive easement."

The campers were told they could still park beside the road where the signs are located, but nothing, not even a can, can be on that triangular piece of land, otherwise it will be deemed trespassing.

The police have just left.

It's still dark and drizzly. It looks like any activities tonight will be scratched.

DAY FOUR
Tuesday, August 9, 2005

Day four began with Cindy Sheehan appearing on *Good Morning America*.

It was a rainy day in central Texas, at times coming down hard. Rumors persisted about the possible arrest of Cindy Sheehan predicted to occur on Thursday.

11:45 a.m. Deborah Mathews reporting:

The weather report from Crawford is that it is nasty, seventy-one degrees and constantly drizzling. A documentarian from Germany is shooting with a bag around her camera. There's lots of water standing everywhere.

Cindy Sheehan is currently in an undisclosed bed and breakfast in Crawford, conducting phone interviews and is expected back at the Peace House or camp area around 1:30 or 2 p.m.

The campers have announced that there will be a thousand crosses erected in the ditches near the campground tomorrow. The crosses have been ordered and a truck left this morning for twenty-four-hour delivery. The crosses are being provided by a Veterans for Peace group out of Louisiana.

"We are looking for volunteers" to help put them in, noted Wilson, explaining that law enforcement personnel might be standing behind them pulling them out as fast as they are erected.

Dick Underhill, the Austin chairman for Veterans for Peace, has issued a call for all veterans to come back to Crawford and support Cindy.

A Secret Service agent showed up a little while ago and was talking to some members of CodePink. He was wearing blue jeans and a windbreaker. When the documentarian from Germany pointed her camera at him from about fifty yards away, he positioned his face away from the camera.

Every five minutes a DPS trooper drives by. It appears that they are on some sort of rotation.

The triangular area where the campers were evicted yesterday, standing in water, now has a no trespassing sign posted.

Although unconfirmed, the campers said that a couple of farmers came by earlier and one said, "You have made your point. Why don't you leave?" Note was made that there is some talk about the entire road being closed if the campers don't leave, which would make it difficult for the farmers to have access to their property from the road.

Sheehan and about six others spent the night in their tents. Somebody brought a pavilion tent and placed it over the sleeping tents. Otherwise, they said, they would have slept in the rain.

DAY FIVE
Wednesday, August 10, 2005

W. Leon Smith recollects:

Problems at the newspaper office in Clifton added to the pleasure of this publisher's working back-to-back "all-nighters." Juggling staff had been a problem, since *The Record,* the sister paper to *The Iconoclast*, had to be composed and put to bed on Wednesday, and it takes staff members to do this.

The Crawford updates were using most of the manpower that should have been devoted to *The Record*. Not to mention that portions of the updates consisted of photographs, which required "working": captioning, and uploading, adding more to the workload as deadline pressure on the other paper mounted.

Then there was the internet.

When I, as publisher of *The Iconoclast,* posted an explosive Kerry endorsement editorial in September 2004, the amount of traffic to the website maxed out the bandwidth, which is shared by other businesses and patrons of the service provider, as well. This meant a slowdown in response when individuals logged on, and posed the potential problem of putting everything at a standstill.

A makeshift solution was eventually reached last year to help with the excessive consumption of bandwidth and to keep information flowing, but there was nothing in place to provide for the onslaught of Sheehan web-surfers who were pushing the website access to the limits. Overload was again fast approaching.

To remedy the situation, I contracted with another service provider and posted a redirect to that site, so that we wouldn't be shut down, even temporarily. But it took time and some doing, while we were critically on deadline for *The Record* and running behind in production.

It was late Tuesday night. I decided to make a trip to Camp Casey myself to obtain a night-time photo of the camp, something which we did not yet have, and perhaps interview someone about how it feels to camp in a ditch.

There was lightning in the distance and the ground was wet from a cloudburst earlier in the day. My college-age daughter, Allison, accompanied me to shoot some photos.

We arrived around midnight on Tuesday. It was dark, save distant lamps here and there. We walked around and eventually ventured toward the main part of the camp. Although you could hear crickets chirping, there was an overlay of quietness in the muggy air.

I had heard that Hadi Jawad, a director at Crawford Peace House, had been spending some time at the camp, so it was him I was seeking to interview.

Next to the road near a supply tent were two people sitting in lawn chairs. The darkness of the night hid their faces as they sat in silhouette. I said, "Excuse me, but have you seen Mr. Jawad?"

The woman, seated on the right, answered.

"No, he's not here tonight, but can I help you? I am Cindy Sheehan."

After introductions, we talked a little while. Sheehan

soon left, and I interviewed her guest. It was a tape-recorded interview, conducted at 12:35 a.m. I posted the story online around 5 a.m. after going back to the office, transcribing the tape, and writing the story. I felt the interview was important in that it explained the battle in which Casey Sheehan died:

Bill Mitchell, Whose Son Was Killed Same Day as Cindy's, Flies to Texas From California to Offer Support
Iconoclast Publisher Makes Midnight Visit to Camp Casey

By W. Leon Smith, Publisher, *The Lone Star Iconoclast*

PRAIRIE CHAPEL ROAD—A distinct calm permeated the grounds of Camp Casey as the midnight hour slipped into Wednesday morning. Crickets sang amid the backdrop of trees on one side, as lights from Waco in the far distance on the opposite side outlined the open prairie in between.

The camp was dark, save the predictable flicker of a thunderhead in the south and the occasional light-up of a cell phone that doubled as a flashlight for a few human night owls seeking a place to get comfortable.

An intermittent sweep of drizzle kept the air muggy, but cool. A few tents and numerous graffiti-scribbled signs were silhouetted as they jutted up from the grass.

In all, about fifteen vehicles had made their way to the sanctuary in the ditch where fate decreed an icon of peace take her stand.

Cindy Sheehan was seated in a lawn chair next to a friend who had come to Crawford to lend support for her cause. He, too, had felt the pangs of losing a child to a war in which he did not believe.

It had been a long day for Sheehan, whose voice

had softened in the wake of seemingly endless interviews. With worldwide attention focused on her quest to expose the war in Iraq as ignoble, the press had become a constant companion.

But she was tired and it was late; and the unknowns of tomorrow would require strength, so she hugged her friend good-night and wandered toward her tent.

Her friend was weary, too, for California is a long way from Texas and the trip had been exhausting. He agreed to visit awhile with the publisher of *The Lone Star Iconoclast* to explain his interest in supporting Cindy.

Bill Mitchell, of Atascadero, California— a city that lies along the central coast halfway between Los Angeles and San Francisco—said that he came to Crawford to support Cindy Sheehan, with whom he holds a special bond.

[Bill Mitchell speaks with W. Leon Smith, publisher of *The Iconoclast*.]

MITCHELL: My son, Sergeant Mike Mitchell, was killed in Iraq on 04-04-04 in the same battle with Casey Sheehan. My daughter connected up with the Sheehan family shortly thereafter. I was in Germany at the time with my son's fiancée. I started e-mailing Cindy when I was in Germany.

ICONOCLAST: Were you in favor of the war prior to his death?

MITCHELL: In February 2003 there was a worldwide rally against the war and I was in San Francisco with 200,000 other people carrying signs and marching against the war. This was a month before the war started. I haven't seen war myself, but I am a vet and under-stand the camaraderie and the military mentality.

ICONOCLAST: How are you dealing with this?

MITCHELL: Not very well. My life's been devas-tated. It's been turned upside down. Very few aspects of my life have a similarity to the past. It just kind of churns you up, shakes you out, and drops you off. I'm doing much better than I have been.

ICONOCLAST: Does it help to bond with other peo-ple who have had similar experiences?

MITCHELL: Extremely. Extremely. I come to events like this and I really get empowered from being with other people and working for the cause. I met Cindy shortly after our sons' deaths. We did some military speak-out events together. I realized there was a power in her speaking and in her stories. Even those people who don't agree with the war, or our opin-ions, see this.

We have a certain credibility. We're not someone up there that's just espousing some ideology or some belief. We're victims of this war like many other people are.

ICONOCLAST: What do you foresee happening with the war?

MITCHELL: Unfortunately, I see it dragging on—unless we are able to put a stop to it. I can tell you that I first spoke out eight weeks after my son's death, on Memorial Day. That was my first speaking event, at a rally. I've pretty much been speaking out since then, just telling my story.

ICONOCLAST: What was he doing in Iraq when he was killed?

MITCHELL: Mike and Casey died on the same day. Mike was part of the 1st Armored Division and Casey was with the 1st Cavalry Division. Mike had been in

Iraq for eleven months. He went there in May 2003 after the *mission had been accomplished*. He was there as part of the stabilization force. Up until April 4—eleven months in Iraq—not one soldier in their company had died.

On April 3, my son and all his buddies packed up all their equipment. They were headed to Kuwait the next week because Casey and the 1st Cavalry were the reinforcements that came. This was much different than the Vietnam days. In the Vietnam days, you had maybe a thousand guys flying in every day and a thousand guys flying back, so you had people there who knew the jungle. They had tribal knowledge.

I am relatively confident that Mike and Casey never met until they were in that plane. That picture that was taken in Kuwait on April 7?* Mike Mitchell and Casey Sheehan were in those boxes.

But Mike couldn't tell the new guys how to get by in Iraq—the tribal knowledge you get being there eleven months. For instance, Mike had basic Arabic down.

Forty-five minutes before Casey died, the general from the 1st Armored Division passed over the command to the general in the 1st Cavalry. So this whole uprising took place on the day when they were transitioning from the 1st Armored to the 1st Cavalry.

So what happened on April 4 is that twenty soldiers from the 1st Cavalry got ambushed in Sadr City. Mike spent eight months at Sadr City. These guys in the 1st Cavalry, it was their first day there. They'd never seen Sadr City before. Those twenty guys that got ambushed didn't realize when they drove into the city that there were piles of tires and rubbish and junked cars, whatever, blocking the access back out. These guys were stuck there within the city.

Mike had been out running with his buddy, Carl, and they came back into the camp and there was a buzz going on. One of the tank commanders came to my son and said, "Mitch, I need you to ride loader today, in Sadr City." Mike goes, "I'm with you."

Mike had spent two years at Fort Hood. He was part of the 1st Cavalry when he was at Fort Hood. I'm sure he felt a certain camaraderie to those new guys that had been ambushed in there.

They send young men to war because [young men] think they're invincible. My son thought he was Mighty Mouse. He kind of laughed when anyone expressed too much concern about his well-being. He told his older sister, Terri, he goes, "There's 35,000 of the 1st Armored here. What's the chance of getting me?" Particularly my son being a mechanic. The loader on the tank is a guy sitting there with an M16 machine gun. So that's what my son was doing the last day of his life.

So, eight soldiers were killed that day, seven from the 1st Cavalry, one from the 1st Armored. That was the first death in Mike's company in eleven months.

We were all back in the states, having suffered through eleven months of Mike being there in Iraq and… he was on his way home. He was a week from going to Kuwait, two weeks in Germany, and three months from his wedding date. He had a fiancée in Germany who was just crushed. But I pretty much adopted her and am helping her continue on.

So, anyway, I'm here in Crawford, Texas today to support my friend, Cindy Sheehan. I appreciate what she's doing. I was against the war beforehand. I wish I could sit here and tell you how much you should appreciate my son for your liberty and freedom, but, you know, I didn't believe that before the war, and when my son died I surely couldn't grab that and cherish that feeling, because I know it's lies that got us there. We have no reason to be in that country. There's no reason that Mike or Casey or the other 1,800 [American] men and women should have died.

ICONOCLAST: You drove here from California?

MITCHELL: I was going to drive, but I ended up getting a plane ticket because Cindy said, "I need you here now." So I flew down to be here and support her and the work she's doing. She's just incredible.

I don't know whether Americans just have too many distractions or are too busy with their own lives, but, you know, this war doesn't touch that many people in America.

ICONOCLAST: What do you think it would take to fix things?

MITCHELL: The mothers of America to all stand up.

It may take the draft. If the recruiting continues to fall short and they are forced to bring the draft back, maybe that might wake people up. But people aren't affected by it. Sometimes, we'll tell people that our sons died in the war, and they go: "What war?"

Every morning when I wake up, it's—hopefully it's my first thought. If I go through five minutes of the morning without thinking about Mike, and all of a sudden I see one of his pictures hanging on my wall, it's kind of a shock again. I'm really kind of happy when I wake up and I have Mike there in my mind because it's not such a shock, a jolt that you go through again.

He was the baby of the family; Casey was the big brother of the family. It's like a little pebble into a pond. There's a ripple effect. There's brothers, sisters, aunts, and uncles.

One of my biggest fears while Mike was in Iraq

was that he would never see his grandmother again. (*Pause.*) Mike's grandmother had to go to his funeral. She's devastated still by it. My mother's a very senti-mental, a very emotional woman. She's having some health issues in her life. I was afraid she would die before Mike got home.

ICONOCLAST: Is there anything you'd like to add?

MITCHELL: I'm sure Cindy has said it, but we know what it feels like to lose a child—to have a child killed in this war. And we're just doing whatever we can to end it so quickly that no one else has to experience that same pain and devastation, the same upset in their lives.

My life has not been the same since my son was killed.

I have three other daughters. I have eight beauti-ful grandchildren. I was at a very good point in my life. Life had been very good to me. And then this just came and turned it upside down.

I had been hanging out, waiting for Mike to get back from Germany. I was going to jump on a plane after he and Bianca had a few weeks together, fly to Germany, spend a few weeks with him, travel around Spain and Portugal a little bit.

I was back to Germany in August, for Mike and Bianca's wedding and the only other plan I had in my life at that point was Mike and Bianca coming home for Christmas together. Mike was bringing his new wife home.

(*Long pause*)—This is the work I do now—to tell my story and to bring the reality, the pain of this war, back to people in America.

It doesn't so much matter whether I'm out speaking in the name of peace and my son's name or whether I'm out camping having a good time, when I come home to my little four walls, my son's still dead. The death of any child is a devastating event for a parent. A piece of your heart dies when your child dies. So I just want to stop this. I don't want to hear about anybody else dying, American or Iraqi.

When Cindy wrote the couple of quotes about Bush, about him wanting to honor the fallen, I don't want any more blood in my son's name—my son wouldn't want any more blood in his name either. My son was a very sensitive, very caring young man. He'd been with these guys for eleven months. There's a real camaraderie that develops. It was about his buddies. It's not about democracy in Iraq; it's not about freedom and liberty in America. It's his buddies, that develops in a military unit, especially in a war zone.

* * * * *

Nathan Diebenow returned to the update forces on Wednesday, as day five progressed. His early-morning reports dealt with communications of support that Cindy Sheehan had been receiving from throughout the country, which had included a letter from sixteen House Democrats to President Bush urging him to meet with Sheehan. They asked that neither Sheehan nor her supporters be arrested as they continued their vigil peacefully.

While Sheehan was tied up conducting interviews, Diane Wilson was dealing with parking issues and the McLennan County Sheriff's Department.

3:43 p.m. Nathan Diebenow reporting:

A ton of flowers are everywhere. Cindy Sheehan is wearing a blue overcoat and carrying two yellow roses. At the bottom of the stem, it says "Texas Democrat."

Her hat has been signed by a bunch of people.

Cindy said she would do anything to keep Casey out of war, she would take her son to Canada or she would run him over with her car. She noted that Casey said, "Mom, I want to go to help my buddies."

Now there is just one vehicle left in the triangle. Everyone else has moved.

The officer is still talking with some people.

It is a little humid. Crickets are chirping. There are about two to three dozen people consistently. There is a lot of media out here.

Cindy is being transported back to the Peace House and will be back at 4:15. There are no crosses yet. There will be meetings to determine when and where to put them.

The Iconoclast published this editorial pertaining to Cindy Sheehan on August 10, 2005.

— *Editorial* —
Speak to Cindy, Mr. President

Cindy Sheehan deserves a few minutes to speak with President Bush.

Not only is she the mother of a soldier killed in Iraq, she is an icon representing millions of Americans who have serious questions regarding the war.

Part of being a "War President" is listening to constituents at home, even to those who might not agree with policy—especially when these numbers are growing.

It is one thing to cock an ear to foreign heads of state and one's myopic inner circle. But a truly responsible President would expand his input to the working classes, would cross the political aisle occasionally, and would be eager to pay special attention to families who will suffer lifetimes of grief as a result of political decisions.

Granted, President Bush is on an extended vacation.

But life goes on.

As do casualties of war.

Cindy Sheehan has traveled far in her quest for the truth.

The world is watching.

Its citizens will draw their own conclusions.

— Written by W. Leon Smith

(Footnote)

*A controversial photo of flag-draped coffins, taken by a civilian cargo worker appeared on the cover of the *Seattle Times*, sparking a debate over the Freedom Of Information Act.

DAY SIX
Thursday, August 11, 2005

Day six started off with Cindy Sheehan receiving a visit from Viggo Mortensen, who starred in *The Lord of the Rings* as King Aragon.

A report of the day, provided by Nathan Diebenow:

Basically, this morning started off like they have four days in a row—with a local resident around six a.m. driving his car to work from one end of the camp to the other, honking his horn all the way down. Members of the camp have videotaped it.

There is a big media presence again today. About 200 crosses, twelve-inches tall, from Veterans for Peace in California are here and have been installed at Camp Casey on the side of the road where Cindy has been sleeping the last five nights.

Many more people are arriving here to show support.

I talked with Jim Harrington, Cindy's lawyer from Texas, who informed me of the legal situation here. He said that the Sheriff's Department is kind of in a bind because the people technically have the right of way on the road to walk on it, but not on the shoulders, the eight feet easement, so they are letting the people around here stay on the side of the road. There apparently is no easement statute in this county. There have been no First Amendment quarrels out here before.

He also said that, legally, there shouldn't be any problem with the President driving through here and having the protestors here, since basically, she's just a mother wanting to talk to him. He pointed out that there are alternatives instead of moving the campers. Like in previous instances, the Secret Service could patrol with their dogs to make sure there are no crazies. There are alternatives to just kicking people out.

[Memorial crosses at Camp Casey devoted to soldiers slain in Iraq.]

The weather is now, at the noon hour, getting hotter. It was nice and breezy this morning, so much so that one of the pavilion tents blew over earlier. With the rains earlier in the week, there's still some mud and a lot of crickets out here just trying to grab as much moisture as they can. One of the landowners on the encampment side talked to Ann

Wright about a big tire track that pulled up a lot of mud. Ann said to him that they would correct that big mud cut, since he mows it.

In all there are over a hundred people in the general area. A lot were forced to park along a dead-end road, probably a mile and a half away.

Right now, Getty wire service is completing an interview with Cindy. She's scheduled for ten more interviews today, but had at least a hundred requests. As of yesterday, she had done 200 interviews. She's doing fifteen-twenty a day.

There are a variety of crosses. There are Christian crosses and also Stars of David.

For instance, here's a Star of David with a biography that reads: Coast Guard Petty Officer Nathan Bruckenthal, twenty-four, was killed April 25, 2005, while conducting maritime intercept operations off of Iraq.

Here's one with a crescent moon that symbolizes Islam, but no name is on it. According to a spokesman, it represents the Islam faith. The goal is to try to represent every major religion.

I hear a cheer and some applause. What's that? Okay, the Porta-Potty has just arrived.

I understand that Bush is at his ranch right now awaiting his 2 p.m. meeting with Rice and Rumsfeld.

Since there is such a demand by the media for interviews, military families are also being interviewed and expect to be doing that all day.

DAY SEVEN
Friday, August 12, 2005

Nathan Diebenow conducted several interviews during the late evening of August 11 and posted this report after the crack of midnight, at 12:05 a.m. Friday:

People have been visiting at the Peace House. They have been checking their e-mails, calling their relatives in other parts of the world, and celebrating birthday parties.

After receiving a foot massage, Cindy Sheehan retired to the "nap room" a little while ago to prepare for Friday while the rest of the people are talking outside. She just left to spend the night at Camp Casey.

Earlier in the evening, there was a meeting at the Crawford Peace House. The main discussion points were parking and shuttle service from the Peace House and Pirate Field parking lot to Camp Casey.

The organizers suggest that people stop by the Crawford Peace House prior to going to Camp Casey, where they will be directed to the football field parking lot.

By the end of the day Thursday, over 600 people are estimated to have walked through the doors of the Crawford Peace House.

Various gifts were given to the Peace House and supporters of Cindy, a few being six shuttle buses from radio personality Randi Rhodes, free wireless service for the Peace House, a barbecue grill being brought in by a man from Texarkana, and a few cases of beer.

There have been thousands of other phone calls of support, as well as requests for rides from the airport to Crawford. One woman has paid the way for a Navajo activist to come to Crawford, said Kay Lucas, a member of Friends of Peace and Crawford Peace House supporter.

Johnny Wolf, the owner of the Peace House, returned from a meeting with Crawford's new mayor, David Poston, and Chief Donnie Tidmore about securing Tonkawa Falls Park for a rally there on Saturday. The outcome of the meeting was that the Crawford Community Center and the park area have been tentatively granted to the supporters of Cindy for a rally. The officials are checking the schedule for any conflicts, as of this evening.

I interviewed Hadi Jawad, one of the directors of the Peace House, Kay Lucas, a member of Friends of Peace Waco, and Johnny Wolf. I will try to have these ready to post later today. Topics included depleted uranium weapons, the Iraqi constitution, the attitudes of the local Crawford people, and the significance of soccer moms speaking out.

I also just finished interviewing two recent graduates of Crawford High School. They asked that their names remain anonymous. One indicated he supports the President, but both said that they themselves would not want to go into the military because they do not know what this war is about.

10:35 a.m. Deborah Mathews reporting:

There's a lot of excitement at Camp Casey. Law enforcement officers have been swarming the place, getting ready for the Presidential motorcade to pass through the camp on the way to a fund-raiser about a mile up the road, at the

Broken Spoke. The pass-through is expected in about an hour and twenty minutes. Campers will be allowed to stand on the infamous triangular piece of ground while the motorcade passes by. Five highway patrol, three Secret Service in bullet-proof vests, two county officers are seen at the moment. A lot of plain-clothes people not seen here earlier are milling around.

Protestors are being instructed on what types of signs they can carry. For instance, if some want to carry crosses left over from yesterday's planting, the metal portions that are inserted into the ground have to be removed; otherwise, they might be considered a weapon.

One officer said, "You all have worked with us so well, and we want to keep that going."

Looks like they are going to move us all back fifty feet. From 11:50 a.m., then an hour-and-a-half until the motorcade comes back by, no one may leave or come to the camp.

Cindy has been doing interviews this morning, with NBC and public radio, and at 10 a.m. called a press pool. At that time, a man that wrote a book, an Iraqi veteran also protesting, said to her: "Your loss is a drop in the bucket."

11:45 a.m. Deborah Mathews reporting:

The motorcade of about twenty vehicles just passed on the way to the Broken Spoke. The activists chanted "Meet With Cindy," "Stop the War," and "Bring Our Troops Home." The road is blocked off to through traffic. He is due back by about 12:45 p.m. At that time the road will be reopened.

We are on the triangular piece of land.

The passing was very quick, the motorcade traveling fast, forty-five-ish miles per hour, which is pretty fast with the curves in the road, one of which is about ninety degrees. It's just "hotter than hell out here. It's just miserable out here. But everyone is determined—both sides."

Seven or eight Sheriff's deputies were decked out in riot gear, the rest of the law enforcement personnel with bullet-proof vests. They are hot. It is extremely hot and humid out here, windy also.

After the passing, the activists are "hanging around," standing around waiting.

Officers are just standing around.

There were no altercations of any kind. Everyone did exactly what they were asked by law enforcement personnel to do.

It seemed intense, but was quick, a lot of waiting, then suddenly the motorcade came through. The campers are offering water to the law enforcement personnel who are also stranded here.

About 100 people are out here, about a third of which are media, not counting law enforcement that number about twenty.

Many were holding signs, some held them next to the yellow "police line don't cross" tape stretched to bisect the triangle. It was previously illegal, off limits to stand on the triangle, but now it is where the onlookers are ordered to stand. It is unknown whether this will revert back to being illegal after the President's return to the ranch.

The officers remain in heavy gear as they await the return of the President in an hour and a half.

1:25 p.m. Deborah Mathews reporting:

The protestors are lined up again now. They are trying to keep a four-foot distance between them and the yellow police tape. The law enforcement personnel have taken off the riot gear. Everyone is waiting for the return of the President to his ranch. It is extremely quiet. You can hear the wind and the helicopter.

Cindy will be standing separated from the rest, so that she will not blend into the crowd.

There's a guy with a squirt bottle of cold water squirting the back of the necks of everyone. He's telling them: "If you don't want to be squirted, raise your hand."

1:35 p.m. Deborah Mathews reporting:

Cindy's lawyer is with officers at the tent, the chopper is still circling, but a lot lower. The motorcade is expected momentarily.

Here comes another police car. Here comes the motorcade led by six highway patrol cars. They are traveling fast. Here they come. I see the motorcade.

Cindy is holding one of her crosses in her left hand in the direction he's coming. She's simply holding it. Her lawyer whispers something to her. She's holding it up high. "Meet With Cindy" is being shouted in unison. The motorcade is not moving as fast as it did last time it came through this area.

The chanting is getting louder. There are a lot of people in these vehicles. Chanting even louder. There's some chicken noises "cluck, cluck, cluck" by protestors. Now, quickly, the motorcade has passed. Cindy told someone that she saw Laura Bush in one of the cars.

People are starting to disburse. Get all your trash off the triangle someone yelled. Cindy Sheehan is being interviewed again. "We want to show him there are people who oppose him. This is real democracy. There are real people that really oppose him," Cindy said.

Cindy is walking toward her tent, walking under the awning, putting the cross back and in the ground, and is sitting down.

Officers with the highway patrol and county are still out here. The Secret Service have moved away and are getting back in their cars.

People are picking up trash where the line was and people are being moved out of this area.

7:50 p.m. Nathan Diebenow reporting:

PRO-BUSH GROUP ARRIVES AT CAMP CASEY

A group of about fifty pro-Bush demonstrators from the Metroplex armed with various sizes of American flags, as well as banners and posters, arrived directly across from Camp Casey on county right-of-way around 6:30 p.m. Radio personality Mike Gallagher, who organized the event, led the group in patriotic songs, a prayer, pro-Bush rhetoric, and thankfulness that they could openly express their beliefs in America. At one point they chanted "We don't care, we don't care."

The group, which traveled in a charter bus and several cars, stayed about thirty minutes and departed for Pirate Field in Crawford to see about another rally. There was no suggestion that they were going to camp the night.

The group was comprised of young and old, from elementary-school-age children to World War II veterans. The only time the group had much contact with the supporters of Cindy Sheehan was when it crossed a line of McLennan County Sheriff's Department vehicles to place American flags beside the crosses that were earlier placed in the ground by supporters of Veterans for Peace.

Sheehan's group held up a banner that said, "Support Our Troops, Bring Them Home Now," sang a song, but remained quiet and respectful during all the time Gallagher's people were there.

I asked Mike Gallagher if he was going to place a flag in front of Casey Sheehan's cross at Camp Casey. He said, "We wanted to. But the police said don't go over there, so we are placing flags over by the white crosses."

Lisa Fithian of United for Peace and Justice said, "We're not going to stop it, you know. If they want to bring American flags, they can place American flags. They're honoring those that have died."

Chief Deputy Randy Plemons, after conversing with a

supervisor, said, "No one was stopped or told not to go over there and place any flags or anything like that. That was not the case here today."

There were Secret Service agents present, along with Sheriff's Department deputies. As I left, there were still at least fifty pro-Sheehan people present. There were bouquets of flowers beside about fifty of the crosses, and a ton of crosses lining the side of the road for about a quarter of a mile.

DAY EIGHT
Saturday, August 13, 2005

Week two began on Saturday, August 13, with coordinator Ann Wright complaining about fair play when she spoke with *The Iconoclast's* Nathan Diebenow:

"There are about fifty Republicans here walking the mile-and-a-half up the road from the Broken Spoke Ranch to Camp Casey. They get to walk on the road. They put us in the ditch, but those who support Bush get the road. I don't understand that. It is so hot and these people are planning to walk all the way. We're here at the Peace House now getting ready for the rally in the park at noon."

12:25 p.m. Nathan Diebenow reporting:

I drove into Crawford, Texas off 317.

The first thing I see is a Carter Blood Drive going on at the Masonic Lodge, people with motorcycles and flashy sports cars lingering outside.

I drive a block or two farther and bikers are on the corner of Spanos' Coffee Station. Signs on the corner say: "Stay the course."

I drive through town. Kids are on bikes riding around. One

is driving a riding lawn mower on the street going downtown. There's a lot of activity at the Peace House, cars parked.

I turn into the parking lot area to the park. There are some flags by Pirate Field, military style, counter-protestors. Driving farther, there's a red Chevy truck coming toward me with a sign saying, "Texas is Bush Country," playing hard rock music.

I park, and from the looks of it, there are a lot of Texas license plates, anti-Bush bumper stickers, Texas Democrat stickers, Howard Dean stickers. A couple of windows have shoe polish print that say, "Talk to Cindy." In all, there are about 200 cars around, and 300 people.

I hear a loud "Welcome to Crawford from people at the Cindy Sheehan rally."

The rallyers "boo" for the President. There are a lot of children in attendance, elementary-school-age and up.

I just talked with a college student, Ansel Herz, who is passing around a petition on the Sudan genocide. The organizers here talked about not petitioning and keeping the message on Cindy.

"I think Sudan is serious enough to gather signatures," said Herz. "I am definitely behind Cindy all the way." He said he watched the interview on *Democracy Now*. From that, he said it is obvious she is speaking from her heart.

I talked to Dawn Farrell, thirty-five, of Grapevine, who works at an accounting firm. She was holding a sign that had Bush giving the middle finger (an outtake from TV that was not aired at the time he did it) and below the image the sign says "Warmonger." She said that she thinks Cindy is going to stay and Bush will not meet with her.

Other posters I'm seeing say: "War's not the answer." "Real Texans don't hide." "Why aren't your daughters fighting in Iraq?" "Denver Moms for Peace."

I spoke with the woman holding that poster. DeAnn Major has one child and is an advocate for people with disabilities.

She drove down here from Denver alone, noting that it took fifteen hours. She said she tried to get some friends to come, too, but one of them said "no" because her car didn't have any air conditioning. She said there was a lot of rain and traffic during the trip, but that she is hoping to come down next weekend for another rally. She said, "I think it's going to gain momentum. I don't care if it takes fifteen hours. If this is the beginning of the end of the war, then I have to be here. I can't wait for my friends to come with me. I'm on my own."

There's a Veterans for Peace guy handing out T-shirts.

Before the rally, people were conversing. It was a pleasant atmosphere.

At 12:09, a helicopter circled overhead. Some think it might have been a Secret Service helicopter.

1:48 p.m. Nathan Diebenow reporting:

People are leaving the rally at Tonkawa Falls Park. They are putting pink and yellow ribbons on the antennas of their cars. License plates include Virginia, Colorado, Arizona, and Missouri.

The Crawford police have stopped traffic along the road leading to Camp Casey. The pro-peace rallyers are stuck there awaiting the arrival of the McLennan County Sheriff's Department. It is hot in the cars. I was allowed to go through, being press, to the Peace House to talk more about what happened.

Three times during the rally, there were helicopters circling. Again, they did not look like media helicopters.

Speakers at the rally included members of Veterans for Peace, Gold Star Families for Peace, Military Families Speak Out, and Iraq Veterans Against the War. Speakers included Ann Wright, Dante Zappala, Hadi Jawad, David Cline, Barbara Porchia, Celeste Zappala, Lietta Rugger, Linda and Phil Waste, Tim Goodrich, Beatriz Saldivar, Jean Prewitt, Sheri Glover, and Sue Niederer.

There were also two female musicians who performed folk and blues music.

Celeste Zappala said how proud she was of her son, Sergeant Sherwood Baker, the first Pennsylvania National Guardsman to die in combat since World War II.

Sue Niederer of Pennington, N.J. said, "Bring the troops home now and take care of them."

She thanked Cindy Sheehan for making Crawford "our home for the month of August." She noted that there were twenty-five families with Gold Star Families for Peace at the rally and she encouraged the people at the rally to attend the September pro-peace events in Washington, D.C.

She had two questions for President Bush and his supporters: "Why aren't Barbara and Jenna Bush fighting in Iraq?" and "Why don't the children of others who support this administration's policies join this war?" Niederer said that she "hoped to hell" that the draft is coming and said that she would personally like to see if any children of Bush supporters would enlist in the military.

Phil Waste of Hinesville, GA said that these are not traitors here, as suggested by right-wing media pundits over the course of this week. He and his wife have three sons and two grandchildren, a grandson and a granddaughter who are active military. In total, they have spent over fifty-seven months in Iraq.

This afternoon, one of the singers will perform at Camp Casey and another rally will be held. They wanted everyone who hasn't seen the Arlington West crosses from Los Angeles to see them. They were created by Veterans for Peace members.

The pro-Bush contingency is right outside Pirate Field in the parking lot, carrying around large American flags. They number about fifty people, including a man with a loudspeaker on the back of a pickup truck.

About 300 people were at the pro-peace rally.

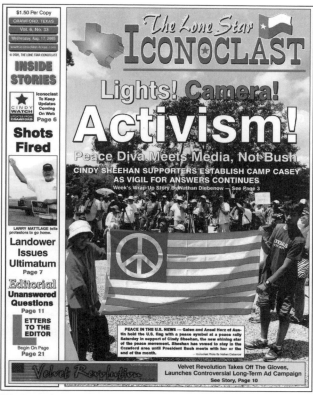

[*The Iconoclast,* Vol.6, No. 33, August 17, 2005.]

5:35 p.m. Nathan Diebenow reporting:

The pro-Bush counter-protestors left Houston at 5 a.m. and arrived at Crawford around 10 a.m. at Camp Casey. The event was organized by members of FreeRepublic.com.

Marine mother Gale Muskiet of Houston estimated that there were 400 in her group that lined up in support of Bush hoping to catch a glimpse of him as he drove on Prairie Chapel Road. The group left there reportedly after 12:30 p.m. for the parking lot of Pirate Field in Crawford. Many of the members of the group had to walk halfway because of traffic congestion.

The 400 estimate has, however, been disputed by others present, who say that the number was considerably less than that.

At the counter-protest rally four Marine moms spoke in support of President Bush and the war on terrorism, saying that the United States must stay the course and that their children chose to join the military of their own free will.

There was a member of the group that dressed up like the Statue of Liberty.

The military moms present were Gale Muskiet, Julie Swain, Ann Semien, and Linda Prince.

When asked if more counter-protest groups will be coming this week, Muskiet said, "If she's willing to continue on her campaign, I would hope the American people would say enough is enough and take a pro-active response."

Linda Prince of Centerville questioned the use of the memorial crosses at Camp Casey with the names of the servicemen who died in Iraq because not all of them or their families would agree with Sheehan's views on ending the Iraq war immediately.

Dr. Raoul Deming, a member of FreeRepublic.com, called the pro-peace demonstrators "un-American" because, he said, "the host organizations are communists with ties to terrorists."

DAY NINE
Sunday, August 14, 2005

10:15 a.m. Deborah Mathews reporting:

SHOTS FIRED!

Camp Casey is becoming very organized, with how-to signs placed about. Ann Wright said, "That's what we are trying to do."

Let me read you the schedule posted on a tree: "9:15 camp meeting; 10 a.m. inter-faith service, 10:30 a.m., Food-Not-Bombs Breakfast at Peace House," and...

Wait! Someone is firing a gun.

(Pause)—He fired it into the air about five times. He appears to be a local inside the fence line on private property. Now he has thrown what looks like a shotgun into the front seat of a pickup, and he's stomping off out of sight. I wonder where he went.

Now he's coming back out. I'm out here standing on the road. He's got a no parking sign in his hand, walking toward his fence. I'm going to go try to talk to him. I've got to hang up.

(Three minutes later)—I went over and talked to the man. He is Larry Mattlage, who says he is on his property and just posted a no-parking sign.

Wait... now there's some Secret Service and cops. I'm going to get closer to hear what they're saying. People in bullet-proof vests are here now. Two Secret Service agents are now walking up his driveway towards his house, with Mr. Mattlage. A member of the Sheriff's Department has arrived. Mr. Mattlage is waving his arms now. All of them are now walking back this way.

Now they are between the lane and the house. He's at the fence now. Let me record what they are saying. I'll call right back.

[Irate local landowner Larry Mattlage imploring protesters to leave.]

11:15 a.m. Deborah Mathews reporting:

Okay, here's what happened.

At 9:15, campers met for a camp meeting to discuss the schedule for the day and ideas for other ways to, "Build this outside of Crawford," said a supporter. The discussion centered around how to progress with Camp Casey. I listened to people ask questions like, "I will be leaving tomorrow and tell me what I need to do when I get home to carry on Camp Casey?" Coordinators responded with, "Make sure you stay in touch with your local law enforcement—follow any regulations pertaining to your area—and we really appreciate it."

Some were given instructions like, "On your way home, make a sign with our supplies here and display it in your window for all to see."

People were asked again to keep the camp clean—even cigarette butts must be picked up. "We want to be respectful of the land and we don't want anyone to have any complaints with anything out here," said Ann Wright.

Other supporters asked questions like, "What can we do to get families involved. We want to get kids on site."

Ann Wright spoke of the parking and location to people. "Be sure to stay off the grass that's marked park only where designated, please. We have this ditch here and here," she said as she pointed to appropriate parking locations. "The ditch is all that we have for this wonderful, tremendous movement."

One supporter, dressed in an outfit of red, white, and blue said: "I can be patriotic and against the war, too. I can't imagine Bush's inhumanity. We have to listen to who is hurting. We have never supported this war and we really need to get our troops home."

As I walked to my car to call the office with an update, I heard a popping sound. When I turned around, I saw a man with a shotgun aimed upward. He looked over his shoulder and then back and fired more shots. Even though I was only about twenty feet from him, it took seeing him with the gun to realize what I was hearing. He put the gun into the cab of the pickup and walked back to his house without saying anything.

He fired the gun from inside his fence line—well within his property; his name is Larry Mattlage—which is across to the east of Camp Casey. He did not fire anywhere but into the sky, away from the camp.

I walked over to the fence line to take a shot of the pickup with the Keystone Light box and the American flag in the back and saw him coming back out. He came to the truck again, took out a sign, and walked to the fence where I was standing. As he hung a "No Parking" sign on his fence, he said:

"We're gonna start doing our war, but we're gonna' do it underneath the law, or whatever it takes. So you all go find you another place to do whatever you're gonna' do, because this is our front yard and backyard."

I asked him, "When you say you all, do you mean the protestors?"

He answered, "I'm talking this whole damn country is neighbors and friends and this is our country. And if this group says that they are so much in Jesus and neighbors' rights and all that they pretend to be, why don't they show it. You gotta' live it. You gotta' live Jesus Christ. And this is not Jesus Christ…"

Another reporter walked up and asked, "Are you Mr. Mattlage?"

"I sure as hell am," he answered. "Well, I want to get on the Letterman Show. I want to get on Jay Leno. This is a joke out here… This ain't about Democrats and this ain't about Republicans. This is about my rights and these people's rights as American citizens who live here. You done your deal. You done your show. Now move on. I'm asking that as an American citizen and a taxpaying citizen, because I pay taxes to the middle of this road, and I mow it, and I keep it clean, and all I got now is trespassers. If that ain't right, it ain't right, but I want the whole world to know what they've done. They started out doing right and now they are doing wrong. When they first got here, I understood their cause and I appreciate it. I don't like the war no more than anybody else, but right here we got war… right on my front yard. Everybody here is sick of it. If everybody will leave now, everybody will go home a winner. Then the President can enjoy his vacation like everybody else and these farmers and ranchers can go check their cattle without having to go through a campsite."

ICONOCLAST: Are any of them prevented from getting to their cattle now?

MATTLAGE: Ma'am, who wants to wade through all these people walking around there. What this is is a war of Porta-Potties and the one with the most Porta-Potties is gonna' win and you know who that is don't you. You all got started out going to the bathroom in a five gallon bucket. Now, I see three Porta-Potties. How many more Porta-Potties are we going to have to put up with? Now, George Bush has more Porta-Potties than you all, so if I was a bettin' man, I'd say he's gonna win. So let's don't make this a little more ridiculous than it is now. Everybody go back a winner. You've made your point. I'm proud of you. God bless all of you.

ICONOCLAST: Did you fire a shotgun?

MATTLAGE: Yes I did! I got a right to fire up in the air. I am getting ready for dove season and you all are messing up my dove huntin', so if you all could please leave and go somewhere else, this whole community would be behind you.

ICONOCLAST: How many acres do you have?

MATTLAGE: It don't make any difference. That don't have nothing to do with it. I pay taxes to the middle of this road and that person over there *(he said as he pointed across the road to the opposite side)* pays taxes to the middle of that road.

ICONOCLAST: So this is your land right here?

MATTLAGE: This is my land right here. We've been here for 125 years, okay. And this group ain't running us out. Our family's fought in wars, drought—grew up without any water—we're pretty tough folks. We will survive this. This group is like Frosty the Snowman here. It's gonna' melt and they'll be back another day. We are just waiting for Frosty to melt. We've got one group over here that's not gonna' give up and we've got one group over here won't give up and we right here in the middle. Do you understand? This ain't New York and it ain't California and it ain't Washington. I'm not political. I'm just a taxpaying citizen that wants my rights. That's all I got to say. Thank you. And I will be back here all night long and I'll be shootin' at doves in the air, so anybody that camps here better get ready for some gunfire. If we don't hit anything, I want every redneck in Texas to come on my property and this property here and we gonna' really have a show. Thank you.

Mr. Mattlage turned and walked back in the direction of his house. Both Secret Service police and the McLennan County Sheriff's Department showed up to talk with Mr. Mattlage. The men went into his gate and they spoke together for a few minutes. Mr. Mattlage then turned and walked back in the direction of the media waiting at his gate.

MATTLAGE: What we have here is we got the Secret Service here and the Sheriff. The Secret Service has got all the power, but they don't have any rights to get rid of this stuff. The Sheriff's Department has got the law which means, they said that we have no rights because they can't stop this. So we've got two law enforcement agencies and all these helicopters up here and none of them can do nothing and will do nothing.

ICONOCLAST: Larry, why did you shoot the gun?

MATTLAGE: Well, I'm getting ready for dove season and you all are still gonna' be here, I'm practicin'.

ICONOCLAST: Was there another message involved in the gunshot?

MATTLAGE: You figure it out for yourself.

ICONOCLAST: Are there any laws…

MATTLAGE: No, in Texas, you can shoot… I ain't threatening nobody. I ain't pointing a gun at nobody. This is Texas.

ICONOCLAST: What do you want them to do Larry?

MATTLAGE: Well these people don't know what to do *(pointing at the Sheriff and the Secret Service)*.

ICONOCLAST: What do you want them to do?

MATTLAGE: When they first came out here, I was sympathetic to their cause, right. They as American citizens have a right to march to protest. It is like this—it's like having company, if you have your brother-in-law at your house for five days, wouldn't it start stinking after a while. You are ready for him to go home, aren't you? Five weeks of this is too much. We live here. It's our community. Apparently we have no respect over here and we have no respect over here. Somebody has got to get together and clear it out. It's a damn shame. The news media has got to solve this dilemma. But we got a dilemma here. We got a battle of the Porta-Potties. You all got started out going to the bathroom in a five-gallon bucket. Then they moved one Porta-Potty in here. Now we got two Porta-Potties. And now we have three and if this keeps up, it will be all the way down the road. And they've got more Porta-Potties over there (pointing at the Bush ranch). The only one winning here is the one cleaning the Porta-Potties.

ICONOCLAST: Now, what are they doing that you don't like?

MATTLAGE: Sir, this community is a tight-knit community. This is a German community of farmers and ranchers who settled this land 145 years ago. We have fought a lot of battles with drought and everything else. This is a tough group of people and they want to just mind their own business. There is nobody said nothing here right now, because

73

they're not that away.

ICONOCLAST: How has your life changed since your new neighbors...

MATTLAGE: Well you can answer that question yourself man. You're standing right there watching it. That's changing my life. Where are you from? Do you want somebody to put this in your backyard? Huh? Or your front yard? This is our yard right here. We just happen in Texas to have a bigger yard than they do in Maryland.

ICONOCLAST: They said that they would leave if the President came and spoke with Cindy, do you support...

MATTLAGE: Sir, I've lived here for six years since the President have moved here, okay. I don't even know him and he's my neighbor. I love him as a neighbor. I don't care what he does, that ain't my business. I ain't a politician. All I know is that when he gets done with the presidency, he is our neighbor and all of you all and all of this protest is out of here. The Good Book says you love your neighbor so I love George Bush. He will be our neighbor as long as we're here then he becomes a part of our community.

ICONOCLAST: What do you say to the fact that these people are just temporary neighbors? Would you love them just the same?

MATTLAGE: I loved them for a week. I mean, would you want somebody invading your house for a long time and blocking your view and blocking the road? I wake up every morning to this stuff. I go to bed every night and got a campground down here on a public road that I'm taxed to the middle of this road. The Sheriff's people down there says that I don't have no rights, but I am paying taxes. The man over there is paying taxes to here. This is how it is in Texas. So, actually, I can't prosecute nobody for trespassing and the Sheriff knows it so he's allowed them to park on my property—my own damn Sheriff—allowing them to park on my property.

ICONOCLAST: Well, what do you want him to do?

MATTLAGE: It's all about respect. Where has common courtesy gone in America? Somewhere, you supposed to respect people. I respect them and I respect George Bush. I can't do nothing about the world situation, okay. Somebody has got to settle. And that's what I'm saying to you people, so the whole world understands my position. I'm not a negotiator.

ICONOCLAST: Those folks down there, they're not used to being out here, understand. This is not their neighborhood, and then you shoot a shotgun in the air and scare them. Did you take that into consideration?

MATTLAGE: I was shooting a bird. You missed it a while ago.

ICONOCLAST: Understood, but can you see where they might get scared that you're shooting a gun in the air?

MATTLAGE: Sir, what I'm afraid of is if this thing don't get settled—these neighbors out here are upset—I don't want nobody getting hurt. I just want 'em to pack their damn tents and go back to where they came from. Their plea is over with. What disturbs me in thinking about all of this is George Bush really wants this going on because that's probably helping his effort in the war. I don't know strategy, okay. I know one thing, they made their point and everybody understands it. How many times do you have to tell people? I feel for that young lady. She's hurting. I know she's hurting. But there are people hurting in this whole community. All of you are hurting because you're leaving your family, coming out here filming this mess. Everybody got a problem. Everybody got a problem and I got one right now. How we resolve it, I don't know. If I could get George Bush over here, I'd get him in a minute. The President can't go talk to everybody that's got a problem, okay. He got other work to do and I understand that. Let me ask you, what are you all going to do about it *(he was asking the press)*? 'Cause you all are part of the problem, too. You all come out here in a car, which you are blocking the road, which if this lady up here that's eighty-five years old, if she has to go to the hospital, the damn ambulance can't even carry her to the hospital. Now, is that any respect? You tell me? That's all I got to say about that.

ICONOCLAST: Larry how do you spell your name?

MATTLAGE: It's on the mailbox.

Mr. Mattlage turned and walked back into the direction of his house, still inside his fence line. He spoke with the law enforcement there a moment more and they moved to come out to where the press waited as he went inside his barn.

Afterward...

The McLennan County Sheriff, Larry Lynch, came outside Mr. Mattlage's gate and spoke to the reporters, saying:

...stay on the right of way and don't impede any traffic while these folks are trying to take care of their business out here. There's nothing we can do.

ICONOCLAST: What about shooting a gun?

SHERIFF: He's on his own property. He's getting ready for dove season.

ICONOCLAST: What would have made that a violation?

SHERIFF: If he had aimed over there. He can't shoot across the road like that. He's on his property, so he's fine.

ICONOCLAST: Did you visit with him about using some restraint or...

SHERIFF: Of course I did. Everybody needs to use restraint in this situation out here. This is a situation that's taken all these folks by storm and it's impacted the way a lot of businesses run out here. So far, everybody has complied and that's what we're here for. The deputies are here, to make sure that this continues on in a peaceful manner. The folks have got to comply with all the rules and regulations and laws of the state of Texas and McLennan County and that's what we're here to tend to this morning.

ICONOCLAST: How long can these people camp out?

SHERIFF: There's no rule on that. There will be some issues brought up at the Commissioners' Court next week.

ICONOCLAST: How about shooting a gun so close to the President's property, anything there?

SHERIFF: No.

ICONOCLAST: The people said that they're worried, they got scared; they called and said that they didn't get a response...

SHERIFF: We responded.

ICONOCLAST: You did respond.

SHERIFF: Look around you son. Look around you and see that we responded. Don't say that we didn't respond. That upsets me.

ICONOCLAST: I'm sorry. That's what they told me...

SHERIFF: Well, check your facts. Just look around you. Whenever there is a violation of the law or a potential violation of the law, this department and everybody else around here is going to respond. Don't say we don't respond.

U.S. Representative Maxine Waters of California visited with Cindy Sheehan on Sunday, bringing a fruit basket and water for all. She presented Sheehan with a bouquet of flowers.

DAY TEN
Monday, August 15, 2005

It had been nine long and difficult days for the staff of
The Iconoclast. It had taken all night Sunday to put to bed
the print edition and now it was almost time to produce
The Clifton Record. Everybody was behind.

To make matters more difficult, the newspaper office
had become an information center for people throughout the country wanting to know the goings-on at Camp
Casey.

Newspapers, magazines, and television stations were
calling, asking that we provide them with spot reporting
from the scene, which we acquiesced to do. At times, they
wanted to interview me or one of our reporters. This takes
a big slice out of the day, but it also provides a chance for
some members of our staff to deal with other forms of the
news media, which is valuable career experience.

Gene Ellis Sills, Ed.D., a regular humor columnist for
The Iconoclast who operates a family ranch in Bosque
County and writes often about the minor catastrophes of
life, was asked to help.

Here is her first report:

11:45 a.m. Gene Ellis reporting:

Activity at Camp Casey is much as it has been for the past few days. Cindy Sheehan held a press conference about 10:30 to discuss the prayer meeting planned for Friday. The supporters at Camp Casey have invited all the local residents to this meeting and hope some will attend.

An unidentified man drove his pickup through the "forbidden" triangle when supporters did not vacate the roadway quickly enough for him to pass.

1:00 p.m. Gene Ellis reporting:

We just had a brief but heavy Texas thunderstorm.

I spoke to a Sheriff's deputy who said everything is pretty calm.

Cindy is holed up in her van talking to some who have come a long way to see her.

At the press conference earlier, Gold Star families spoke first. Beatriz Saldivar whose nephew, Sergeant Daniel Torres, was killed in Iraq, spoke about the importance of supporting Cindy Sheehan. Juan Torres, whose son was killed in friendly fire in Afghanistan, said that those soldiers should be remembered, too. Cindy Sheehan held a Q&A and explained how the event has expanded beyond her original initiative. She said that if Bush would come and talk to her, she would go home.

3:15 p.m. Gene Ellis reporting:

Cindy Sheehan is having her hair cut. The stylist came in from Austin on her day off, knowing that Cindy wanted to have her hair cut.

Cindy mentioned that some recent comments in the media regarding the possibility that she would refuse to speak with President Bush are completely untrue. She still wants to speak with President Bush.

7:45 p.m. Gene Ellis reporting:

Overall, the afternoon has been fairly quiet at the camp, with the usual interviews and plans being made for tomorrow. A camp meeting is slated for tonight.

I have conducted a few interviews with interesting people who have been here and will get those transcribed for posting tomorrow.

DAY ELEVEN
Tuesday, August 16, 2005

Day eleven saw angry Crawford-area residents appeal to the McLennan County Commissioners' Court for removal of the protestors.

9:45 a.m. Deborah Mathews reporting from the courthouse:

Several Crawford-area residents addressed the Commissioners' Court.

Some of the comments were:

"We don't know everyone that's out there, what type of people they are, and we don't think they do either."

"Unsafe situation getting in and out of there. I have serious concerns for the safety of my children. No one can ensure our safety."

"I am resentful of my daughter walking outside and having microphones shoved in her face. She was smart enough not to speak."

"I don't live there yet. My house is under construction. If we let this continue it's just going to get worse and worse. What happens the next time? We don't know the laws, either. When my child waits for the bus after we move, I want to know she's safe."

"We have civil rights, too, and they're being seriously compromised at this time."

In the hallway, following the hearing, some were saying:

"We don't know who to trust. We moved to the country for peace and quiet. It's only a matter of time till someone gets hurt. Who are they getting their point across to now?

"We're just asking to relocate it. We're sacrificing the safety of our children. Theirs is an important issue, but they need to move. We are a strong, German family community. We'll weather this. We're not saying stop; we're saying move."

One of the camp coordinators, Ann Wright, in speaking to the court, said that the campers are trying as hard as they can to respect those around them, following guidelines that have been set out, and want this to continue peacefully.

As this was an amended agenda for a budget meeting, no action can be taken regarding the petitioners.

Commissioner Ray Meadows said: "I will be out there again today when the buses run. I will take care of the road just like any other road I would. What we're dealing with is a liability and a safety issue."

"There's a lot of property for sale there; buy a piece of property," he said when asked about a solution.

"We want to get through this. I want to be able to work with both sides. I feel sure this happens anywhere with any President's hometown. I've been out three times already. I'll be out there again today," Meadows added.

Another staff member of *The Lone Star Iconoclast*, Michael Harvey, was assigned to Camp Casey Tuesday morning and filed this report:

10:20 a.m. Michael Harvey reporting:

Cindy Sheehan is preparing for a 10:30 press conference.

Volunteers have been attempting to repair and replace some of the crosses that were run over by a truck last night. A suspect was apprehended and arrested, but the name is currently being withheld.

10:38 a.m. Michael Harvey reporting:

More on the truck running over the crosses: According to sources out here, the man suspected of running over the crosses with a truck hails from McLennan County and is fifty-nine years old. He was apparently apprehended after he got a flat tire. One of the crosses was apparently stuck in a tire.

According to Diane Wilson, a local landowner has offered one acre on one side of the road and 180 acres on the other side of the road for use by Camp Casey. Although the exact location has yet to be announced, it is apparently closer to the Bush ranch than the current location of Camp Casey. It is being speculated that Camp Casey will be moved soon.

The press conference is about to begin.

10:50 a.m. Michael Harvey reporting:

A couple of guys from Iraq Veterans Against the War talked to the group about how the damage to the crosses desecrated the memory of the soldiers who have died in Iraq.

1:50 p.m. Gene Ellis reporting

It's hot, with about fifty people out here. They have been re-establishing the crosses that were damaged yesterday.

3:20 p.m. Gene Ellis reporting:

It has now been confirmed. Camp Casey will be moved. During an interview with this reporter, Cindy Sheehan indicated that a landowner has agreed to allow Camp Casey to move onto his property, which will put the camp closer to the Bush ranch. More on this as it develops.

5:25 p.m. Gene Ellis reporting:

A McLennan County resident, Larry Northern, fifty-nine, has been charged with Criminal Mischief Over $1,500 and Under $20,000.

Northern has posted bond and has been released. Bail had been set at $3,000, according to authorities.

Yesterday, a pickup truck, with a chain and bar attached, ran through a row of white crosses at Camp Casey, according to eyewitnesses.

The crosses had been erected as memorials to soldiers who had died in Iraq. The exhibit was produced in California and brought to Crawford.

Sheehan, who arrived in Crawford on August 6, has been demanding a meeting with President Bush to inquire about the death of her son, Casey, a 1st Cavalry Division soldier who was killed last year in Iraq.

In a prepared statement, Sheehan said after the mowing down of several hundred of the crosses, "Our hearts are broken about this."

Today, volunteers have been attempting to repair as many of the crosses as possible.

Discussion continues regarding moving the camp to another location. A press conference has been scheduled for 6 p.m. to address this issue.

Thirty-five dozen red roses were delivered to Sheehan from Florida in response to the destruction of the crosses.

6:45 p.m. Deborah Mathews reporting:
PRESS CONFERENCE

Cindy Sheehan held a press conference a few minutes ago. Here is what she said:

"A kind gentleman from down the road offered us the use of his property. It's right by the barricade. He offered it because he heard about the shots fired.

"He didn't think that was right. He happens to be the third cousin of the person that fired the shots and so he came down and offered us his land. We are in the middle of making that happen. We will be moving within the next few days and we are not being forced to move.

"You can ask the Sheriff's Department. We are cooperating fully with them and they are cooperating fully with us. This is going to be a better place. We can spread out. We don't have to lay in the ditch. We don't have to stay in a ditch. And we'll have plenty of room for parking and everything like that.

"We're going to be moving in the next few days. We just wanted to let you guys know."

When asked if it will be safer, she said: "A lot safer, yeah."

"We won't be blocking any roads. There won't be as much traffic. We're going to leave Arlington Crawford over here and leave a few people here to watch it and to tell everybody where we've moved to."

When asked about anything the camp will need at the new location, Sheehan said: "We're going to need tarps... you know, covering, because there's not as much shade over in that place."

At the conclusion of the press conference, Cindy Sheehan received a private phone call and walked across Camp Casey to be alone. Someone from the counter-protest area immediately came close to where she was and held a cross high in the air.

DAY TWELVE
Wednesday, August 17, 2005

As Cindy Sheehan's vigil reached the approximate halfway point, activity at the newspaper office was brisk. We were again on deadline with *The Clifton Record* and I had been very busy taking care of city business, also being Clifton's mayor. Again, I was facing a twenty-four-hour workday and the staff in the office was disoriented, what with the constant phone calls regarding Cindy Sheehan and the swell of interviews sought of our staff members.

9:35 a.m. Deborah Mathews reporting:
CONFERENCE WITH FRED MATTLAGE:

Local landowner Fred Mattlage held a telephone press conference this morning at 8:30 to explain his reasons for donating land to Cindy Sheehan and Camp Casey.

"I wanted to provide this property as a place where they could peacefully assemble," he said. "This was an act of compassion to a mother who's lost her son."

Mattlage is a fifty-two-year-old self-employed small business owner who resides in Waco. He is a distant relative of Larry Mattlage, the man who fired the shotgun into the air on Sunday.

The property he is offering is co-owned by his brothers Karl and Mark and sister, Patricia. Brother Mark actually owns the one acre tract where the new camp site will be. This one acre is at the corner of Prairie Chapel Road and Camen Church Road. Directly across from the one acre, the Mattlages own a 212-acre tract, which they will make available for parking purposes.

The 212-acre tract is to be opened today at 10 a.m. by Mattlage. He is asking that Camp Casey supporters have a person at the gate of the property at all times due to the fact that there are cattle on the site. Gates will have to be kept shut.

Mattlage went on to say, "These people did not approach me at any time. I went to the Peace House in Crawford to offer the land, but it is not my desire to put them in closer proximity to the President. I only want to alleviate some of the problems with the residents."

Mattlage also said, "The gun shots [by Larry Mattlage] did not play into my decision. This has nothing to do with family."

When asked about any parallels to his own time in the military service—1972-1974 with the 82nd Airborne Division of the U.S. Army—Mattlage responded with, "There really is no comparison, but our country should have a good reason to commit our boys to combat. Maybe we didn't learn a valuable enough lesson from Vietnam."

Mattlage said that he is not really a supporter [of Sheehan or the President] either way. "I don't really agree with the policy of being in the war."

Mattlage has had no contact with the White House.

A camp supporter said, "It is unlikely that we will move today. We are using this time to figure out how to best begin the move. We need to get some shade up first. The plan is to begin moving by the end of tomorrow or early on Friday, before our interfaith meeting."

2:45 p.m. Michael Harvey reporting:

The Iconoclast staff has been attempting to draw up a rough map showing how to reach the new Camp Casey.

Members of the Texas Coalition for an Independent Judiciary met at the Crawford Post Office Wednesday morning to send empty boxes to the White House. Coalition members called on President Bush to fill the boxes with documents from Supreme Court nominee John Roberts' record as a deputy solicitor general in the first Bush administration.

Phone Interview With Ann Wright of Camp Casey:

"WE NEED LOTS AND LOTS OF TRAFFIC CONES AND ROPE!!"

Camp supporters are currently discussing options for the big move to the one acre patch of land. "We're excited about moving. I think this is the closest [that protest] has been to the White House. We will be right next to a Secret Service checkpoint," said Wright.

Supporters are encouraged to use the shuttle out to Camp Casey, as parking remains a problem.

Earlier reports were of a donation of 212 acres across from the new campsite to be used for parking. That offer has changed and campers will be restricted to the one acre; however, a very large tent will be erected to provide the shade that this new site doesn't offer. Also, Wright explains: "We are bringing in trailers to help with interviews and so forth. There will be bathroom facilities and cooking facilities as well."

This morning, we were told that the crosses ("Arlington West," the campers have come to call it) will in fact be moved to the new site. Wright said, "We have evaluated the best area where the most impact will be made."

9:30 p.m. Gene Ellis reporting:

Tonight, candlelight vigils have been held throughout the country in support of Cindy Sheehan. In all, at least 1,380 vigils were scheduled. Responsible for the push were Move On, True Majority, and Democracy for America.

Plans are under way for an interfaith service on Friday at Camp Casey. Coordinators at the camp are expecting hundreds, perhaps thousands, to attend and are encouraging people to travel to Crawford for this special event. It is scheduled for noon on Friday. Religious leaders of all faiths have a special invitation to attend.

Arrangements continue to be made regarding the move to Fred Mattlage's property.

It has been announced that activist/singer/songwriter David Rovics, who was featured in a previous edition of *The Iconoclast*, has recorded "Song for Cindy Sheehan."

The Iconoclast published this editorial on August 17, pertaining to Cindy Sheehan:

— Editorial —
Unanswered Questions

There once was a word.

It was called "accountability."

It meant that when a tragedy or mishap occurs, truthful answers would naturally follow.

The requisite for truthful answers extends beyond the "why." It is a mechanism geared toward avoidance of the same tragedy again.

Cindy Sheehan is seeking answers, as are Americans throughout the nation.

The administration's answers relating to America's involvement in the war with Iraq keep changing, open proof that lies have been told.

The recently unearthed Downing Street Memos take it a step deeper, indicating that a hidden agenda existed prior to day one of the involvement.

Then we learned of the illegal ouster of an agent who was poised to blow the lid off the "fixing of facts" aimed at devising an untruthful reason to go to war.

One thing is a fact: Soldiers who die or are injured while serving under the flag of their country are patriots, having made an ultimate sacrifice, and should be always honored for this.

It is the venue of politicians to assure that the expenditures of these lives are minimized and that the political reasons to activate a military into aggression are solid, sincere, and a last resort.

This is the basis of one mother's complaint.

However, accurate answers and the attached motives remain hidden, as untruths have already been exposed.

"Faith" is an acceptable virtue when forfeited to a supreme being.

But even faith requires questions, for without them, it is worthless, blind.

Remember President Reagan's motto when dealing with the nuclear arms race and the Soviet Union: "Trust must verify."

"Facts" are the required measure on the world slide rule in assuring the accountability and motives of a politician.

Yet unanswered questions prevail within this administration—even beyond those related to the war in Iraq.

These, too, might be asked of the President:

- With this country so severely in debt, why did you grant tax cuts to the very wealthy?
- Why did you attempt to undo our country's Social

Security system and why did you go back on your pre-election promise to not raid the Social Security trust fund?

- Why did you develop plans, and then enact them, to disable fundamental portions of the Constitution of the United States?
- Why did you try to stop the efforts of the 9/11 commission? Why don't you want a full investigation as to what happened?
- Why did you grant no-bid contracts to the Vice President's former company?
- Why have you promoted the export of American jobs overseas?
- Why aren't you supporting the needs of our veterans?
- Why don't you ever listen to or surround yourself with Americans who might not agree with you politically?
- Why was Jeff Gannon planted in your press conferences to throw softball questions to you?
- Why are depleted uranium weapons being used in Iraq?

And there are many more.

But this is the question of the moment:

Why didn't you stop for five minutes on your way back to the ranch Friday to answer Cindy Sheehan's questions? You made time for a fund-raiser, time to throw the first pitch at a baseball game, time to meet with foreign heads of government—but no time to meet with and answer the questions of a mother whose son was killed in Iraq?

This is what "War Presidents" do. There is no vacation from reality.

Ms. Sheehan made the long trip from California to Texas and has spent over a week in the boiling Texas sun, camping as close as she can get to your gate, fending off fire ants, attempting to let you know that she needs to speak with you.

Her quest for your attention is important in that she represents many other mothers who want truthful answers to the same questions.

How hard can it be?

— Written by W. Leon Smith

DAY THIRTEEN
Thursday, August 18, 2005

10:45 a.m. Gene Ellis reporting:

A press conference was just held. Cindy Sheehan was not present, but speaking were Mimi Evans and Medea Benjamin of CodePink and DeDe Miller, Sheehan's sister.

They are calling on a campaign of mothers everywhere to write to Laura Bush and encourage her to influence her husband to end the war. They really aren't anxious for the Bush daughters to go to war. They don't want anyone to go to war, they said.

This afternoon, there will be a meeting at 4 o'clock to write letters. At 5 p.m., the group will read letters that people have written, and at 5:30 p.m., Sheehan's sister, DeDe Miller, will lead a peaceful march to attempt to deliver the letters up the road to Laura Bush.

Last night (about 1 a.m.), an unidentified man showed up at the camp pretending to be newly arrived, which isn't unusual. He was met by Cindy Sheehan's private security people, Patrick Miller from southeast Kansas and Dave Jensen from Tyler, Texas. The man said he worked for Jeb Bush and told Diane Wilson, a camp coordinator, that he could have her arrested anytime he wanted. He indicated, said Wilson, that he knew Secret Service men that happened to drive by.

Tammara Rosenleaf, whose husband is now at Ft. Hood and is expected to deploy within a year, said she knew immediately something was amiss. Buddy Spell, Sheehan's attorney, from Louisiana, chased the man down the road. The man left his car when chased. The car was towed and, according to camp sources, the man is now apparently in custody. Sheehan's security personnel praised the law enforcement officers for their prompt attention to this matter and their patience during the entire stay at Camp Casey.

5:00 p.m. Gene Ellis reporting:

Cindy Sheehan is en route to an airport to go to Los Angeles to be with her mother, who suffered a stroke this afternoon, it has been reported. The letter walk will still be held. About a hundred supporters are at the camp right now (more, counting the media) as letters are being read. Some were received by e-mail from various parts of the country.

5:15 p.m. Gene Ellis reporting:

We have reached the checkpoint and the march was mostly uneventful. They are still singing. There's a lot of law enforcement presence here. People are told to slow down on the road here. Nothing's happening right now. Here's the lady with the basket full of letters. I'll report back in a few minutes.

5:30 p.m. Gene Ellis reporting:

The latest on Cindy Sheehan's mother: According to camp coordinator Ann Wright, all they knew at the camp was that Cindy's mother suffered a stroke this afternoon. They don't know her condition. Cindy is taking a flight to Los Angeles to be with her and will return as soon as she can. Sheehan's sister, DeDe Miller, went with her.

The march to deliver letters to Laura Bush has begun. The walk is about 1.7 miles in the "hot Texas sun." Marchers are utilizing the road because the ditch was full of media trucks.

I am in front of the marchers taking photographs and notes. The marchers are singing old favorites like "Ain't Gonna Study War No More," and are chanting "Give Peace a Chance."

Now they are singing "Down by the Riverside," but have altered the words, like this: "Gonna Give These Letters to Laura Bush, Down by the Riverside."

The marchers are carrying a big letter in front of the group that reads:

"Dear Mrs. Bush, We as women of America appeal to you to understand the urgency of our plea.

"We cannot abide the continued loss of precious lives on both sides in Iraq.

"Our plea is simple. Please, read our letters and ask your husband to meet with Cindy Sheehan who represents so many military wives and mothers."

About a hundred marchers, plus the media, are in line. It is led by two Sheriff's Department cars, then the procession, complete with long banners.

Now they are chanting, "Hey, Hey, Ho, Ho—the Iraqi war has got to go." Marchers are carrying umbrellas. It has to be close to a hundred degrees, but there is a breeze. That helps. The road is hot, though.

It's now 5:42 p.m. I'm with Lieutenant Sid Franklin of the McLennan County Sheriff's Department. He has decided that the group should not march all the way to the checkpoint, because of the heat and safety factors with traffic. A shuttle will be used. The marchers traveled about half-a-mile on foot prior to this decision being made. Lieutenant Franklin and Sergeant John Kolinek with the Sheriff's

Department have done a wonderful job, according to camp coordinators.

It's now 5:46 p.m. There's been a change in plans. The marchers decided to walk and not take the shuttle. The officers say they were concerned since the thermometer in the squad car reads 98 degrees and, with the heat index and the heat from the road, they suspect that the actual temperature is about 108 degrees for the marchers.

6:30 p.m. Gene Ellis reporting:

The letters were accepted by a young man named Bill Burck who says he is a member of the staff secretary's office. He said it was a pleasure for him to accept these letters to be delivered to George and Laura Bush. Medea Benjamin, who carried one of the three baskets that were delivered, said the group was appealing to "President Bush's better half," because she's a mother and they thought she would understand and appeal to her husband on their behalf.

The group is planning to shuttle back to camp. It was a very peaceful delivery of letters.

DAY FOURTEEN
Friday, August 19, 2005

With the absence of Cindy Sheehan at the camp, it was clear that some of the spark had vanished, but the remaining supporters acted as congenial troopers and worked hard to prepare for her return.

9:00 a.m. Deborah Mathews reporting:

I spoke with Diane Wilson who told me that there are three tents up at the new campsite—the huge tent (about 60 x 180), the cooking tent, and Cindy's tent. She said that there will be a lot of cooking.

There is also a trailer there that was donated for Cindy's use. Moving is still in progress and the coordinators hope to have completed the majority of it by this evening. Moving will stop during the interfaith meeting to be held at noon.

Wilson mentioned a man who is a friend of Martin Luther King—someone who marched with him—will be at the interfaith meeting today and they are expecting some singers also.

She did say that Joan Baez will be there on Sunday.

She also mentioned that the phone reception at the new

site is poor. She wondered if it wasn't due to the proximity to the President's ranch.

There is no update yet on the condition of Cindy Sheehan's mom who suffered a stroke yesterday.

The Iconoclast has processed photos from yesterday's march to the checkpoint near the Bush ranch. Letters from mothers wanting an end to war delivered three baskets of letters addressed to Laura Bush.

1:40 p.m. Gene Ellis reporting:

Coordinators at Camp Casey just received a phone call from Cindy Sheehan. Cindy says her mother is going to see some specialists this afternoon. Cindy said that her mother recognized her and squeezed her hand, but could not speak. Cindy is penciled in to return to Crawford on Sunday, if she can.

8:00 p.m. Gene Ellis reporting:

Ann Wright, coordinator at Camp Casey, says that the entire camp is deeply saddened by the health affliction that has befallen Cindy Sheehan's mother.

"This is a tragic part of life that she is having to go through while dealing with national and international issues," said Wright. "Her family comes first, and her extended family here will carry on with her mission to see the President. There are other Gold Star families here with the same concerns, and they will carry on until she is able to return. There will be no slowdown in our activities to highlight the war and its tragic consequences. I urge the President to meet with the families to explain why we must be at war with Iraq."

Wright also praised the State of Texas and said those at the camp had been treated with the greatest respect here.

Two prayer vigils were held this morning. At 8 a.m., supporters of President Bush, American troops, and the mission of Iraqi freedom held an "I GIVE A SHEET" vigil, prayer rally, and breakfast at the Crawford Community Center. Over thirty-five sheets from Georgia alone were hung up. They were filled with signatures of support for President Bush. The original plan was to deliver photographs of the sheets to the President, wash the actual sheets and donate them to homeless shelters in Texas. However, permission was given to deliver the actual sheets. It is unclear whether they will now be donated to shelters.

A tent is being set up for the benefit of supporters of President Bush and the troops in front of the Yellow Rose in Crawford (at the intersection of highways 317 and 185).

The owner of the Yellow Rose, Bill Johnson, is an acquaintance of President Bush and wanted to provide a clearing house for Bush supporters who come to the area and wish to find out what's happening, how to organize, etc. Johnson said this group is trying to serve God and country. They plan a candlelight vigil for next Saturday, in the evening, around the large angel silhouette on the tent site. They are calling the area Ft. Qualls, in honor of a fallen soldier whose father lives in Temple, Texas and supports President Bush and the war effort.

An interfaith service was held at Camp Casey. Clergy from around the country joined together to pray for the families present, President Bush, Iraqis, and all who are caught in turmoil, including children, Cindy Sheehan, and her mother, who yesterday suffered a stroke. There were prayers for the common good, for unborn children, for widows left behind, even prayers for the press, that they may be courageous and tenacious in finding and reporting events. There were prayers for the leaders of nations and religions to speak the truth.

Pastor Eric Folkerth of the United Methodist Church in Dallas played guitar to open the service, played during the service, and closed with an original song entitled "Prairie Chapel Road," about Cindy Sheehan's time at Camp Casey.

Rabbi Arthur Wasco of the Shalom Center in Philadelphia chanted a prayer that was a plea to "turn us to God," a cry out to God for our children. He also sang a moving and quite well known (among those of the Jewish faith) Hebrew prayer for peace.

Clergy too numerous to mention added their prayers. They were from many places, several from Waco and the central Texas area. The vigil continued with a special service for the families who wished to come to the center and form a circle. This circle was surrounded by more clergy and that circle was ringed by the press and others. It was an emotional moment.

The heat was intense, and there was concern for Father Don Bobb of St. Andrews Presbyterian Church of Austin who was affected by mild dehydration. He was wearing a heavy clerical robe, which was removed. He was given water and tended to by one of the Veterans and several others who happened to be close by. He was feeling much better an hour or so later at the Peace House.

After the prayer service, several of the CodePink members and others from the camp made a second trip to the checkpoint in front of the Bush ranch. They shuttled part way and walked toward the end of the route. Their aim was to deliver a letter to the President assuring him that they would continue with Cindy Sheehan's efforts in her absence and hoped to meet with him.

Secret Servicemen were not able to accept the envelope and the red and white carnations accompanying it. When they were asked by the group if a representative from the President might meet them to accept the envelope, they were refused. So the envelope was left on the pavement in front of the checkpoint, along with the flowers. About an hour later, the offering lay on the hot, dirty pavement, imprinted with tire tracks.

Donna Mulhearn, a member of CodePink, who had arrived from Sydney, Australia to support Cindy Sheehan's efforts, said that Australia follows this event closely and that there are a great number of supporters there. She brought with her many messages and e-mails to deliver to Sheehan and the supporters.

There was a luncheon at the Peace House in Crawford for the clergy, the families, and any other camp supporters who cared to attend. Members of the press were also invited. Tents and trees provided shade for the many tables set up outside.

Both Camp Casey and the Peace House are well stocked with water and often food, as well, for supporters.

Hank Klein from Pasadena, California reported that there is now a bugler at the camp. Jeff Key is a veteran who plays "Taps" every evening at 8:30, which Klein said is quite an emotional event. Key, since his return from the war, has written a stage play based upon his experiences. This play has been in a small theater in the Los Angeles area and is now headed for Broadway as "The Eyes of Babylon."

Key is being or has been processed out of the military because he came out as gay. He will probably do a reading from his play during afternoon or evening entertainment this weekend.

There is still an unconfirmed rumor that Joan Baez will make an appearance during the weekend, as well might other well-known entertainers. The camp coordinators say the entertainment is for the benefit of the supporters. The general public is not encouraged to attend any concerts or other entertainment that may occur. Parking would be a major problem if large crowds came for the entertainment, it was noted.

There isn't much word on the condition of Cindy Shee-han's mother. Of course, everyone at the camp wishes her a complete and speedy recovery from her stroke.

Buddy Spell of Louisiana, along with the camp coordinators, has assumed a position of authority within the camp in Cindy Sheehan's absence. He works closely with the Sheriff's Department and other entities. Spell and Spell are the legal counsel for Sheehan and the camp. Great care is being taken to assure everything is done within the law. He and his wife and law partner, Annie Spell, have been camping with the supporters for much of the last two weeks.

There has been talk in Crawford that neighbors of Camp Casey are upset because of all the trash. However, during the last four days, at least, all refuse has been picked up and disposed of daily. According to camp coordinators, there is a great effort among this group to leave the area as it was found.

[Marine sergeant and Iraq veteran Jeff Key playing "Taps" at Camp Casey.]

DAY FIFTEEN
Saturday, August 20, 2005

10 a.m. Michael Harvey reporting:

So far, there is not much activity this morning. There are about seven counter-protestors across the road from Camp Casey and seven McLennan County Sheriff's deputies present also. Cindy Sheehan remains with her mother in Los Angeles, California.

A performance stage is being set up at Camp II and cooking equipment is being placed there.

Here is the schedule posted for today:

SCHEDULE:
8:00 Clean up
8:30 Camp Meeting
9:30 Peace Keeper Training
1:00-4:00 Peace Keeper Training and Camp Meeting
4:00 Catered meal at Camp II
7:00 Music at Camp II, featuring Steve Earle and
    James McMurtry

Perry Jefferies has supplied a new map depicting

the camps and has offered to share it with *Iconoclast* readers.

4:20 p.m. Gene Ellis reporting:

People are continuing to arrive at Camp Casey II, where a large tent has been erected.

This reporter just finished conducting an interview with Ken Gordon, majority leader for the Colorado Senate.

Camp Casey coordinators reported that last night there were many cars and tents in the ditch at the old camp-ground. Currently at Camp Casey II there are about 250 people under or near the big tent. There is guitar music in the background, and it is fairly hot at the site.

6:45 p.m. Gene Ellis reporting:

Regarding the condition of Cindy Sheehan's mother, there is guarded optimism. At this point, it seems that the stroke may not be as serious as was feared. Cindy is hoping to return on Sunday, but nothing is definite.

The original Camp Casey is not going to be dismantled. The Vets and certain other supporters are planning to remain in that location. Families, especially families with children, will spend much of their time at the new camp that is in a field rather than in a ditch. Much emotion has been invested in the first Camp Casey, and many do not want to leave. A support group has been established there, and the same is expected to happen at the new camp.

Camp coordinator Ann Wright said, regarding the new location, "President Bush can't leave his ranch without passing one of the camps on the way out." Wright was in the military for twenty-nine years and in the Foreign Service for another sixteen.

There are still unconfirmed rumors of the Sunday arrival of Joan Baez and other well-known actors and per-

formers both tonight and Sunday. These celebrities who
will be entertaining the Sheehan supporters do not want
publicity, are giving their time to show their support and
are there in solidarity.

DAY SIXTEEN
Sunday, August 21, 2005

12 p.m. Gene Ellis reporting:

It has been a relatively quiet morning at the two Camp Caseys. There have been frequent tourist-type visitors and a large number of media representatives present.

Buddy and Annie Spell have departed the camp. They have been in charge of some of the areas and have provided legal service, including interacting with law enforcement personnel on behalf of the camps.

It is very hot in central Texas today.

As events unfold, photos and further reports will be published.

6:45 p.m. Gene Ellis reporting:

Activity at Camp Casey picked up this afternoon with a variety of entertainers providing music.

Currently, about 400 people are at Camp Casey II.

Folk singer Joan Baez arrived here about an hour ago and is staying in a trailer, awaiting her performance at a concert later this evening. She gave a short press conference upon her arrival.

Also to perform tonight is King Flip, a rapper who is a native of Memphis, Tennessee. and has been living in Berlin.

It remains very warm at the campgrounds with activity picking up.

DAY SEVENTEEN
Monday, August 22, 2005

We apologize for our scant update reporting yesterday, but things at the camp went from "not that much reportable," to everything happening at once, which took more time than usual for us to produce.

The big news was the entertainment at Camp Casey II, which featured some top performers.

True to rumors, Joan Baez did indeed appear.

[Peace activist Joan Baez, during her performance at Camp Casey.]

Interview With Joan Baez
By Gene Ellis

I was able to interview Joan Baez after her first Camp Casey II performance. She left the stage, spent quiet moments with both veterans and Gold Star mothers and family members, hugged them, cried softly with them. In an impromptu moment, she joined Jeff Key as he blew "Taps" before crosses in the moonlight. When he finished, the hundreds of supporters present were completely quiet. She whispered to me as we returned to the trailer, "Is it always like this?" And I answered, "Yes."

Ms. Baez returned to the area behind the trailer, spent a silent thirty minutes in a dark corner of the field. She appeared exhausted from the emotion of the evening, sat at a table in the moonlight, laid her head in her arms, and wept. Time was needed to process the intensity of the evening's events. Then she graciously agreed to an interview for *The Lone Star Iconoclast* in her trailer, although she still seemed somewhat overwhelmed.

The next day, when asked if she had ever experienced, during the protests of the sixties and seventies, anything like the previous night at Camp Casey II, Ms. Baez answered that she hadn't experienced anything quite like it at any time during her life.

Baez had planned to stay for a day. But she remained for a week, long enough to meet Ms. Sheehan upon Sheehan's return to Crawford. This was significant. Cindy Sheehan had left (to visit her ailing mother) before Joan Baez arrived. Baez, the legend, kept things on track and provided a focal point during Sheehan's absence. Then the Queen of Folk stepped gracefully into the background (if such a thing is possible), to become just another supporter, when Sheehan returned.

ICONOCLAST: This is Joan Baez, having her dinner!

BAEZ: This is Joan Baez, recovering from the evening's events, if it's possible. As I said, I had my ticket before I got invited.

ICONOCLAST: You've come a long way since "Silver Dagger." Do you think this is anything like the beginning of the Vietnam protests?

BAEZ: It sure feels like it. I don't know if you can predict those things. They don't come very often. With Cindy, what happened was Cindy dropped the last tear that made the thing happen. There is always some catalyst. Martin Luther King, for instance, did things he didn't want to do... I haven't met Cindy yet. I'm going to stay in order to meet her.

ICONOCLAST: Do you see any differences you would like to discuss between the protests of the Vietnam War era and what you see happening now? Or is it too early to tell?

BAEZ: It's too early to tell, but I know one thing. Meeting two black families tonight is an interesting spin. It was very much a white protest movement back then. It's in the hearts of the mothers now and it's not going to matter what ethnic or racial backgrounds they have.

ICONOCLAST: There have been some Hispanic families here, as well, with whom I've spoken. Someone suggested I ask why you came, but I decided that was a stupid question.

BAEZ: I got one stupider. A reporter from CNN asked if I was still politically active. (*Laughter from both of us*). I thought, "You dope!"

ICONOCLAST: As long as you can breathe, right?

BAEZ: I was sitting there being interviewed about Cindy. It was funny.

ICONOCLAST: So you will continue to protest this

war in Iraq through your art, through your singing, through your voice?

BAEZ: Well, yes. You know, I have these women to thank for giving me a platform and an opportunity to sing. I have my own platform when I travel. To be in on something so extraordinary as this is really a gift.

ICONOCLAST: How is life for Joan Baez in 2005? We've watched you a long time, happily.

BAEZ: It's interesting. My son got shorted out for a lot of years because I was traveling. I wasn't there every day. Even if I were in town, I wouldn't be much help at night. I missed a lot. I was caught up in other parts of my life. There was also a lot of promiscuity.

I have taken time now to be with my son and my granddaughter. I live with my mother, who is in her nineties. I like having time to talk to people and take a lot more time just for myself. I enjoy being outside. I sleep in a tree, a tree house. I take things a bit slower. We had an early flight, and live an hour and a half from the airport. So last night, I set the alarm for a quarter past five to get it moving.

ICONOCLAST: Will we hear your performance tonight as part of a live performance album, do you think?

BAEZ: No. I was singing so badly.

ICONOCLAST: Oh you have no idea how good it sounded. It was wonderful.

BAEZ: I'm glad you say that. I haven't played the guitar in a long time. I only picked it up again about a week and a half ago. (I'm going on tour in September). My fingers were like spaghetti.

ICONOCLAST: I don't believe anyone noticed that but you.

(At this point, Ms. Baez, who had had a very long day, began to appear tired. I felt it would be considerate to cut the interview short).

ICONOCLAST: I thank you very much for the interview, on behalf of *The Lone Star Iconoclast*. Everyone is so grateful to you for being here. I personally feel your presence lent much importance to Ms. Sheehan's cause. I thank you for your time.

* * * * *

12:20 p.m. Gene Ellis reporting:

Information provided by camp officials is that Congresswoman Sheila Jackson Lee will be speaking at Camp Casey tonight. Plans are for her speech to begin at 6:30 in the tent of Camp Casey II.

4:22 p.m. Gene Ellis reporting:

Ann Wright announced that Joan Baez was so pleased to be a part of this and had asked Wright to give her an excuse to stay. As a result, Baez will provide a personal view of the history of political activism during the last forty years. There will also be entertainment.

At 10 a.m., Ms. Baez was having quiet conversation with individuals or small groups—different groups of the Gold Star Families—around one of the tables that have been set up under the big tent at Camp Casey II. She is wearing a hat that was given to her by *The Iconoclast*. The newspaper also gave her a tee shirt.

Brad Friedman of Brad Blog is up and running and interviewing. He interviewed Jeff Key, the Iraq war vet who has been blowing "Taps" every evening at Camp Casey I. Last night, with Joan Baez at his side, Key performed "Taps" at Camp Casey II. After the interview with Key, Ms. Baez became available, so Friedman interviewed her.

Tammara Rosenleaf said: "At this time, the information they have is that Cindy Sheehan won't be back before Wednesday, at the earliest. We have no updates on the

THE VIGIL 26 DAYS IN CRAWFORD, TEXAS

condition of her mother."

It really is hot! There are concerns over providing proper care to some people who have experienced symptoms of dehydration. People are being urged to drink water. Coordinators are closely watching campers' water intake.

Coordinators are seeking an *ambulance with a driver*.

It has been said that older people are not as easy to rehydrate as younger, often requiring IV fluids. Coordinators have the equipment to deliver IV fluids at camp. People are urged to bring hats and drink a lot of water. There is water available.

Tammara Rosenleaf said, "Camp I was closed to new campers arriving over the weekend because the line of cars and tents was getting so long that they were concerned over safety issues. Most of the families with children and the families and individuals who are just arriving now will be camping at Camp Casey II."

Things have been quiet and uneventful all last night and today; particularly at Camp I. At 4 p.m., just a few people were to be seen milling around.

Donations are pouring in from all over the nation and used to pay rent on the huge tent, food, and other necessary items.

Later:

Joan Baez gave the first half of an informative and entertaining personal history of political activism of the last forty years. She also sang between each segment of the story. She'll be completing her lecture within the next few days at a time to be announced.

There is a busload of Bush supporters from military families slated to arrive in Crawford this weekend. The group is called Move America Forward.

Baez continues to grant interviews during her stay at Camp Casey.

DAY EIGHTEEN
Tuesday, August 23, 2005

10:30 a.m. Gene Ellis reporting

Brad Friedman of Brad Blog's "Operation Noble Cause" got up and running at the Camp, broadcasting. Today, Brad's first guest speaker at noon will be actress Margot Kidder.

Joan Baez is still at Camp Casey and gave a speech last night on an account of "Her Life in Activism." This speech will be continued tonight at Camp Casey. Baez was introduced by Congresswoman Sheila Jackson Lee.

Very few people were at Camp Casey II this morning, but more and more are arriving as the day progresses. The weather is very hot and there was one incident of a woman having some mild dehydration. Extended forecasts have suggested that it is likely to be very warm in central Texas during the next few days.

Dennis Kynd, a member of Veterans for Peace, will be arriving tomorrow at Camp Casey and will be speaking at a time to be announced.

Brad Friedman continues his afternoon live radio broadcasts from Camp Casey II, where he is providing updates to what is happening there as he conducts in-

THE VIGIL 26 DAYS IN CRAWFORD, TEXAS

terviews with people in attendance. Yesterday, he interviewed Joan Baez.

1:20 p.m. Gene Ellis reporting:

Singer Joan Baez will be at Camp Casey until at least Friday morning.

Tonight, there will be a candlelight vigil held by Gold Star Families and Military Families Speak Out (MFSO) at Camp Casey II. It will honor both the families of the fallen and the fallen. The idea behind it is that Cindy Sheehan has lit a candle of hope and the groups want to continue to light more candles of hope. The Reverend Emilee Whitehurst, a Presbyterian minister from Austin, will preside. Ms. Baez should be there this evening too, but it is unclear if she will continue with the history of peace activism.

9 p.m. Gene Ellis reporting:

Ann Wright, camp coordinator, attended a meeting at the County Commissioners' offices held today. There have been requests by some county residents who want a countywide ordinance to close more roads in the area near the two Camp Caseys. If they are successful in their request, it would affect parking at both camps. No word yet on the outcome of the hearing.

It is very hot in the tent at Camp Casey II, despite the shade it provides. It seems there is more of a breeze at Camp Casey I. Some Camp Casey supporters continue to cool off at "the swimming hole," a natural pond at a park near the Peace House.

Parking during the early morning hours is light at both camps. Later in the day, it is recommended that visitors park at the Peace House and take one of the many shuttles to the camps.

Twenty-five veterans are arriving tomorrow at Camp Casey I on the White Rose bus, the bus on which Cindy

Sheehan first arrived. They want to keep the original message going. Dennis Kynd will also arrive and speak at a time to be announced.

Various groups with related concerns have joined both camps. There has been some discussion as to the possibility of setting up another, smaller tent, so these groups may be separated from the original sponsoring groups.

The Peace House volunteers have been doing an outstanding job providing food, water, and other non-alcoholic beverages to visitors to the Peace House and Camp Casey II. The supplies are purchased with donations. The preparation is provided by volunteers. Food Not Bombs rolled into Camp Casey I last week in its bright blue van and started feeding Sheehan supporters there.

There is a now a well-organized Artists' Check-In Tent at Camp Casey II. All persons hoping to provide entertainment should stop in as they enter the camp. Lauren Sullivan of Lawrence, Kansas is the volunteer coordinator for the camp.

Patrick Miller, a veteran from Moline, Kansas and the man on duty the day Gary Qualls removed his son's cross, has been working with traffic control and security at Camp I. He reported that both days and nights have been quiet lately. However, today the Bush supporters on the other side of "The Triangle" played loud recordings of Rush Limbaugh. Miller praised the McLennan County Sheriff's Department deputies for they wonderful job they have done from day one.

At 5:30, there was a planning meeting for the peaceful protest to be held Wednesday at the VA Hospital in Waco to urge the government not to close VA Hospitals around the country. The deputy mayor of Waco and a representative from Congressman Chet Edwards' office are scheduled to attend. Anyone planning to caravan from the Crawford area can meet the group at 11:15 on Wednesday morning at the intersection of highways 6 and 185 (in Speegleville). There is a Ranch Branch Bank (First National Bank of Valley Mills) on the corner.

There was vandalism sometime late Monday night to a large pro-Bush sign on the side of the Yellow Rose in Crawford, the unofficial pro-Bush headquarters in the area. A small, Hitler-type moustache was drawn in black on the face of the man.

Several crosses of deceased soldiers said to have been removed by disgruntled widows or families from the line of crosses at Camp Casey I have been placed in front of Camp Qualls, the pro-Bush tent. The pro-Bush group claims that Cindy Sheehan supporters have repeatedly replaced the names of those fallen soldiers whose families have asked that their loved ones' crosses be removed. The pro-Bush group is displaying the duplicate crosses in question. The names include Qualls, for whom Fort Qualls is named, as well as Ernest E. Utt, Robert C. Thornton, Kevin A. Cuming, Sean P. Sims, and James Bekstrand. There is at least one other cross standing with the group that seems to have been added by a family member who simply wanted his son's name to be displayed on a cross at this location.

Jim Goodnow of Veterans for Peace from Terlingua, Texas is part of the team that tends to the crosses at both camps. He said the requests to remove names are honored immediately, and that no names have been put back once there has been a request for removal. He said the paper containing the name is simply removed from the cross and another name put in its place. The crosses were not, to his knowledge, ever given to family members.

DAY NINETEEN
Wednesday, August 24, 2005

As coverage of the Sheehan story extended itself into day-after-day reporting, it became apparent that not all members of *The Iconoclast* staff thought it was a good idea.

Don M. Fisher, who helped start the paper, took exception to the layout of the online front page and much of the content pertaining to Cindy Sheehan, and said so—strongly—in his weekly "Call to Mind" column:

— *Editorial* —
We're *The Iconoclast*, Not Just Another Pretty Face
By Don M. Fisher

As Uncle Hugh used to say, "Never try to speak for somebody else. Unless, of course, you're usin' them as an alias."

It was embarrassing.

To watch Cindy Sheehan's transition from a grieving mother to a political clown was pathetic.

To have taken part in that made-for-TV demagoguery, even to the limited extent that I did, is repugnant to me.

The Iconoclast's histrionic pandering to these theatrics was dishonest, prejudiced, and self-serving.

We crossed the line, fine though it may be drawn, between sympathetic observer and propagandist.

When we changed our news focus, or rather had it changed for us, we determined that we would seek out stories that do not earn play in other venues. We did not, and promised ourselves we would not, promote any cause, movement or point of view. We would merely be certain that those who did advocate such had a non-discriminatory, or, in the extreme, sympathetic forum for their ideas.

That does not mean an uncritical forum; that does not mean unreasoned proselytizing.

I was appalled at the "Cindy Watch" or "Support Cindy" or similar links on our web site. Not that those links are problematic for the adherents of this point of view; they just have no place in the editorial content of this publication except as advertisements. They were not labeled as such, and should have been.

Moreover, the tone and tenor or *The Iconoclast*'s copy was clearly doctrinaire.

We became the mirror image of the intellectually narcissistic fascism that has become the broadcast standard in this country.

For about a week now I have felt like I needed a bath.

There are two issues that involved me in this perpetual error in news judgment.

First, there's the event.

The real value of Cindy Sheehan's vigil has been largely ignored.

Prior to the Cindy Circus, Neighbor Bush had been successful in keeping the First Amendment at bay.

As governor, he successfully ensured that only pro-Bush demonstrators were seen in front of the governor's mansion. He kept that up in the White House, and even had demonstrators beaten in Oregon during his second campaign.

Until a few days ago, the Secret Service had kept anyone away from the public right-of-way around the Bush Pile, restricting demonstrations to a park miles away from Little George.

The President of the United States, any president, gets paid to put up with demonstrations against his will.

It goes with the job.

Yet we have concentrated on the show, on the woman herself.

She certainly paid for the right to call Neighbor Bush to task.

She had the opportunity to do that once and blew it, probably because of that thin veneer of civility that keeps us all from each others' throats on a daily basis.

But now, after reflection on everything she wished she had said at that first meeting, she does not really want to talk to the President.

She wants to urinate in his Post Toasties.

Much as we might all like that, we have no constitutional right to do so.

Her personal position might be a little more credible without the sound bites, the PR firm and the celebrity endorsements. She is no longer a grieving mother; she is a marketing scheme, and that leads us to consider why the product cannot simply sell itself.

So when Neighbor Bush said, in effect, "I've heard what she has to say from others, and I don't agree with her," it struck me that he had a point.

And that point was: There is no longer any point to all this.

All the minds that will be changed have been.

George Bush has shown what he is made of, and it is sorry stuff.

He will not listen to those who disagree with him, neither will his blindly obedient myrmidons and neither will those protesting his policies.

And while that is antithetical to everything Americans are all supposed to believe in, the point is taken. End of story. The big boar coon just drowned your best hound and it's a mile back to the truck. Call the fire and piss on the dogs.

Second, there's our part in all this.

I participated in a couple of editorial discussions about this, after which I kept myself at arm's length from the story.

Not that I really tried to get closer. I did consider interviewing Ms. Sheehan, but then, as events unfolded, thought better of it. I have a problem with anyone, even those with whom I agree, asking me to make them the news.

That would have the same effect as interviewing George Bush.

But I feel about the treatment of this story a little as my conscience pricks me regarding the Bush election.

There must have been more I could have done.

As Hemingway once said, "If you're any damned good at all, everything is your fault."

We are all to blame for this war.

We were too silent during the clamor for vengeance after the World Trade Center attacks. We did not shout down the network info-ads billed as the nightly news. We did not throw ourselves in front of the gerrymandering train that gave fascism a permanent majority in the Congress. We have simply not cared that much about this war because the casualties aren't that high, and the absence of a draft brings it into the lives of only a few.

We have allowed a political faction to usurp patriotism and make militarism synonymous with courage.

We kept too quiet then and so have become too boisterous now.

Insofar as *The Iconoclast* goes, we have tried to curry favor, to say what our readers wanted to hear.

We failed you.

It does not matter whether you liked what *The Iconoclast* reported.

We have damaged our credibility, even if you did enjoy watching the wreck.

Frankly, I don't care what you think.

If I do, I am not a journalist. I become a sycophant with no voice and no vision.

And I leave you to face a dangerous world armed with nothing but the sound of your own voice.

* * * * *

In the same edition, my Trenchwalker column hailed Sheehan as an individual who did much to defeat apathy:

— *Editorial* —
Apathy Conquered, Thanks to Sheehan
By W. Leon Smith

Cindy Sheehan will go down in history as the woman who, in a determined, yet soft-spoken, and dignified, manner stoked the fires of debate and made them hotter.

Uneasiness often results in mere apathy.

But to bring similar factions together to speak with one voice requires an icon to lead, and Sheehan has become that.

With both sides of the Iraq issue now embroiled in debate, the United States cannot help but benefit, for overall, it is the people who are taking sides and ordering their political employees to act, not the other way around.

For too long, Americans have withered into complacency, which is a breeding ground for imperialism.

They now realize that one person can make a difference.

They are speaking on the sidewalks; they are speaking in coffeehouses. They are discussing politics in their homes.

They are identifying problems that, prior to the bold and courageous actions of Cindy Sheehan, they felt they could not change.

They now know differently.

They want their President, their Congressmen, and their Senators to come clean.

They want to know why gasoline prices continue to skyrocket.

They want to know why President Bush lied about going to war with Iraq.

They want to know why the federal government continues to eat away at the dignity of the Constitution.

They want to know why the environment is being shortchanged.

They want to know why lawmakers are spending the Social Security trust fund.

They want to know why the rich are getting richer and the poor poorer.

They are tired of being lied to.

They know, thanks to Cindy Sheehan, that the time

has come for America to get back on track and for light to again shine on the so-called American dream.

Now that more than sixty percent of the American people want an end to the war in Iraq, what will our leaders in Washington do? Abide by the will of their employers or continue to hawk our rights to their own special interests?

That is where we are.

Where we go depends upon you.

* * * * *

1:00 a.m. Michael Harvey reporting:

At the candlelight vigil held last night, Lance Corporal Jeff Key, a U.S. Marine Corps reservist, played "Taps" on a trumpet. After a short prayer, Joan Baez sang "Amazing Grace."

Brad Friedman will continue his afternoon live radio broadcast from Camp Casey II today. A group will be leaving Camp Casey II around 11 a.m. and arriving at the Waco Veteran's Hospital around noon to push for continued funding of the facility.

2:00 p.m. Gene Ellis reporting:

Veterans returning to Camp Casey from the protest in Waco at the VA hospital will be served lunch. It's another hot day in central Texas. Supporters are hanging several banners. There is a small crowd right now. It is quiet at the camp, with about fifty people at Camp Casey II.

Camp Casey supporters have provided the following information:

Cindy Sheehan will arrive at the Waco Airport at 4:30 p.m. today. It is anticipated that she will make stops at both camps after her return to Crawford. All public activities will cease at 6:30. She will be granting no interviews today.

A mock helicopter pad is being erected at Camp Casey II to make the point that it should be very easy for Bush to come here and meet Sheehan.

Ann Wright was at a Commissioners' Court meeting yesterday. It was voted three to two to hold a public hearing (TBA) on the resolution as it now stands, which is to restrict traffic and activities on seven miles of road in the Crawford area. The resolution would affect stopping, parking, talking, etc. on these roads.

Ann Wright said: "The two commissioners who voted against the resolution felt it was overly restrictive because it is also bad for the farmers, ranchers, and residents in the area and would affect free speech, free access, etc." She added: "For future protests, it is important to seriously consider these issues."

Wright met with three of the neighbors after the hearing and acknowledged their concerns. Wright called the superintendent of the Crawford schools to go over any ways they might make the situation safer for the children.

"We want to be sensitive to all the needs of the residents and their children," said Wright.

Camp bugler Lance Corporal Jeff Key, Iraq Veteran Against the War, has returned to camp. He shared that he got as far as the Austin Airport, couldn't leave, and had to come back. *The Iconoclast* has an interview scheduled with him later today.

A separate tent is being erected for people with concerns different from Cindy Sheehan's.

With donations that have come in, pro-Bush supporters are gearing up to provide tents and Porta-Potties to anyone who wishes to join them at a site at the last curve before Camp Casey I. They have arranged for these conveniences in anticipation of the large influx of pro-Bush supporters expected this weekend.

7:20 p.m. Gene Ellis reporting:

A plea has gone out for both bottled water and donations to assure the continued supply of water for both Camp Caseys and the Peace House.

For those who care to help, bottled water may be brought to the Peace House or to either camp by arriving supporters, or donations may be made through PayPal or by check.

According to Johnny Wolf, founder of the Peace House, most of the donations have been small. "But there have been so very, very many, we have been able to provide the tent, supplies to provide the meals, the kitchen facilities at Camp II, the supplies for both camps and the Peace House. We have used as many volunteers as possible to stretch the donations as far as we can. If new donations don't come in, by the time Cindy leaves, we expect to be almost bankrupt again."

Another plea was issued by the medical doctor who has been donating her time for the last few days. Dr. Maria Mulligan asks that any doctors, nurses, EMTs, or other volunteers please come for the weekend (or before), as she must leave on Friday.

7:30 p.m. Michael Harvey reporting:

Cindy Sheehan arrived at Camp Casey I to place flowers at the cross of her son. Smiles of welcome gave way to tears of compassion as she broke down at Camp Casey and was overcome by both emotion and the heat.

DAY TWENTY
Thursday, August 25, 2005

11:45 a.m. Gene Ellis reporting:

In her press conference this morning, Cindy Sheehan told reporters that she respects other mothers who have children in the military and acknowledges that each has her own opinion or point of view, but they all should respect the opinions of the rest.

Also speaking was Mark Anderson, national corps manager of the American Friends Service Committee, a Quaker organization that sponsors an exhibit circulating the country. It is entitled Eyes Wide Open, and includes a display of the boots of fallen American soldiers in Iraq. As of today, there are 1,873 boots. Casey Sheehan's boots were returned to Cindy Sheehan who laid them at the cross with Casey's name today.

Mark Anderson reiterated the need for President Bush to define the "noble cause," and said the public wants to be told when he's going to bring the troops home. He said that the President and all congressmen should be held accountable for those who have died in Iraq.

Today, Cindy Sheehan is not granting interviews, but did

tell *The Iconoclast* that her mother is doing better. Cindy Sheehan's sister, DeDe Miller, remained in Los Angeles with their mother.

In all, there are about 100 people milling around Camp Casey II this morning. It is again hot, and a doctor is still here for those needing medical attention.

1:10 p.m. Gene Ellis reporting:

A third-year medical student has arrived at Camp Casey. Dr. Saif Rizvi from Chicago came to the camp as a supporter and was drafted into service as a member of the medical staff. One more nurse has arrived, but those with medical training are still needed.

Camp coordinator Ann Wright said, "The area at Camp Casey II has no camping space left. There is limited space at site I. Those newcomers wishing to camp may have to camp in town or somewhere else."

Wright also said, "Those coming for the activities this weekend, bring your own spray misters or perhaps a wet kerchief—anything you need to help with the heat. The crush of people expected should bring plenty of water. Also, because of the heat, pets should be left at home if possible, due to the heat. Please be watchful of the children and the elderly, as they are more susceptible to the heat."

A bus from Arizona will be arriving this afternoon. Fifteen members of Veterans for Peace will be arriving on Saturday. Five buses from Austin, Houston, and Dallas are expected this weekend. It is uncertain how many others might arrive.

9:45 p.m. Gene Ellis reporting:

Due to the large numbers of people expected to descend on Camp Casey this weekend, the second camp has been closed to tents. The front area must be cleared to accommodate the larger crowds. There might be a limited number of spaces in the ditch at Camp I, but overflow campers must find area camping facilities in Crawford, Waco, and other central Texas campgrounds. A list of area campgrounds will hopefully be compiled. Bob Sutter at the Crawford camping area can only accommodate ten to twelve campers.

According to Ann Wright, camp coordinator, they are thrilled with the number of people wanting to come, but there just isn't that much room. "We couldn't have accommodated any of this if we hadn't been loaned this additional land for Camp Casey II. This has been a godsend."

There have been some problems with the media's lack of respect for the memorials at both camps. Care must be taken to avoid stepping on the area where crosses have been placed and to be considerate of the personal space of those who pause before the memorials. The crosses mean a great deal to the veterans and other supporters, and activists at both camps.

Any additional physicians or other medical professionals who wish to assist at the camps are most welcome. Nurse and licensed massage therapist Jean Lasky of Port Townsend, Washington arrived today to help in the Medic Tent.

During Cindy Sheehan's press conference this morning, she told the media that she will leave Crawford on August 31. She will begin a bus tour of several cities on the following day, and be in Washington, D.C. on September 24 to begin a permanent vigil.

When asked if she felt she had been treated fairly by the press, Sheehan answered, "More fairly than not." She reiterated several points covered before. When asked if she thought she and her supporters had made a difference, she said, "I was just the spark." She does believe it has made a difference and changed things.

Lance Corporal Jeff Key, the Marine and camp bugler,

will stay in Crawford until August 31. Joan Baez is staying at least until Saturday. Baez's arrival and performances kept the spark alive during Sheehan's absence. Now Baez has graciously stepped aside and almost become just another supporter and anti-war activist among many others. She slept under the stars Wednesday night, by the crosses. She was visible this morning as one of the crowd that gathered for the press conference.

Thirty supporters were expected this afternoon from Arizona and another fifteen Veterans for Peace were due in on their traveling bus. The veterans and military families groups continue their presence, mainly at Camp I. Code-Pink moved their headquarters to Camp II when it was opened. At this time, it seems there will be no room to erect another tent to accommodate persons with related concerns, as was earlier reported.

On schedule for this evening was a dinner at 6 p.m. For tomorrow, the only postings thus far are another press event at 10:30 a.m., a peacekeeper training session at 1 p.m., dinner at approximately 6:30 p.m., and movies tomorrow night (if equipment arrives as expected). This schedule is an early version and subject to change

Saturday, buses are expected to begin arriving at approximately 11 p.m. There will be a noon rally in support of Cindy Sheehan. At 2 p.m., there will be a barbecue to which the Bushes have been invited. Everyone is asked to bring an apple pie. The only thing on Saturday's evening schedule thus far is "informal visiting." Again, this is subject to change and will be updated in future postings.

Additional shuttles and volunteer drivers are needed for this weekend. It is possible that the buses arriving this weekend can be used as shuttles, as well.

Lauren Sullivan, the volunteer coordinator, praised the efforts of Joseph, the Porta-Potty pumper. When he arrives, people cheer and clap.

Bush supporter Bill Johnson left his Yellow Rose head-quarters, "Fort Qualls," in downtown Crawford, to lead a 3 p.m. press conference in front of an independent, unrelated (to Johnson) group of Bush supporters across "the triangle" from Camp Casey I.

The group of independent supporters of both President Bush and our troops were dismayed that Johnson chose the site they staked out almost two weeks ago in which to stage his press conference. They wish to make very clear that they are in no way connected to Ft. Qualls or Johnson and do not necessarily agree with his approach.

The independent Bush supporters have used donations to purchase water, chairs, and tents. They have arranged for Porta-Potties at their location across from Camp Casey I, and also at the field loaned for their use at the curve of the road before Camp Casey I. This field will be used for parking, and if necessary, the field directly across Prairie Chapel Road, as well.

The independent pro-Bush supporters have erected signs all along the road directly across from the line of crosses placed as a memorial by the Cindy Sheehan supporters.

According to his group, 2,000 Bush supporters are expected this weekend. Reinforcements will arrive from Georgia, including many of the same people who brought sheets last week for the "I Give a Sheet" program. Buses will arrive from California on Saturday, including the group called "Move America Forward."

The Yellow Rose in Crawford and Fort Qualls enjoyed a steady stream of visitors today, according to reports by the two Bush supporters questioned, but was almost empty at 5:30 p.m. Their schedule for the weekend includes a program called "America Speaks" (Silent Christian Majority) at 11 a.m., grand opening with ribbon cutting on Saturday morning at noon, a twenty-one gun salute to follow, with

"Taps" and bagpipes. It is unclear at this time if guns would be allowed in downtown Crawford for this salute.

Soldiers will be recognized at 12:45 p.m. There will be entertainment at 1 p.m., and a challenge: an open debate scheduled for 2 p.m. It is hoped by the pro-Bush group that Cindy Sheehan will take part, but it is unclear if she has actually been invited to participate at this time or is aware of the challenge. There will be a candlelight prayer service at the Golden Angel at 7:30 p.m.

The weekend promises to be crowded and temperatures will be high. The McLennan County Sheriff's Department, along with other local and state law enforcement officials, will again employ their "zero tolerance" approach. Media can go freely from tent to tent, but law enforcement officials warn caution. They will have their hands full protecting the huge crowds of supporters on both sides of this issue. Additional law enforcement professionals will be brought in to control the crowds and keep everyone safe.

DAY TWENTY-ONE
Friday, August 26, 2005

4:15 p.m. Gene Ellis reporting:

Cindy Sheehan held a press conference this morning. She was joined by three Gold Star fathers. Sheehan asked again how many more must die and said that Iraq was not about defending America. She said that people got off the apathy fence. She talked about the bus tour after Camp Casey to begin a three-week engagement.

There are two new RNs in the medic tent today, four medics available for both camps, and Dr. Jeff Riterman, a cardiologist who came as a supporter is available.

A Native American and Iraq veteran very much against the war was present.

Lunch was served. Ann Wright, coordinator, spoke about the challenges that Sheehan's group will face with the opposition groups or counter-protestors that are expected tomorrow.

The two Camp Caseys and the Peace House are expecting 1,000 to 1,500 supporters tomorrow. Five busloads are expected from Austin, Dallas, and Houston alone. There will be a rally at noon under the big tent at Camp Casey II.

There will be a barbecue later, perhaps at 2 p.m. Wright stressed that "we are a nonviolent group here in a peaceful spirit wanting to speak to our President these last twenty days."

There are some roads that may be closed to the shuttles, but not to other vehicles, tomorrow.

There was a peacekeeping workshop that is just finishing. Johnny Wolf spoke, giving tips on how to keep one's cool.

The Reverend Peter Johnson, of the SCLC, who worked with Martin Luther King, instructed peace-keeping volunteers on the subject of non-violence.

It's very, very hot. There are currently about 200 people under the tent.

6:30 p.m. Gene Ellis reporting:

On Saturday, the population of Crawford is expected to swell by thousands. At Camp Casey II, entertainment on the stage is planned all day. People are being encouraged to come to that location instead of Camp Casey I.

The intense heat and the possibility of clashes between pro-war and anti-war supporters may make Saturday a dangerous day. Caution is being urged and people are instructed to keep their tempers at bay.

DAY TWENTY-TWO
Saturday, August 27, 2005

Saturday was an explosive day, with thousands arriving in Crawford, not only to support Cindy Sheehan, but also to rally against her.

A rally was planned downtown in Crawford near the school district's football field. The event was part of the "You Don't Speak for Me, Cindy" campaign.

The Iconoclast dispatched three reporters that day, with Michael Harvey covering Camp Casey I and its opposition camp across the road, Camp Reality.

Gene Ellis was sent to cover Camp Casey II, while Deborah Mathews was given the anti-Sheehan rally near Pirate Field.

The reports are collated according to time:

11:00 a.m. Gene Ellis reporting from Camp Casey:

There are about twenty state trooper vehicles out here, not including a number of Sheriff's Department vehicles.

Right now, there are about 100 individuals on the Camp Casey side of the triangle and about sixty to seventy on the pro-war side.

On the drive here, there appeared to be about twenty people at the pro-Bush encampment just outside of Crawford.

Law enforcement personnel reported that one arrest has been made at Camp Casey I. A pro-Bush supporter reportedly attempted to harass a Camp Casey supporter during the night and was eventually asked to leave by law enforcement. Then again this morning, officers say the man returned, becoming obnoxious and mouthing off. After the man mouthed off to an officer, the man was arrested and charged with interfering with the duties of a public servant. The man's name has not been released.

Currently, dancing and musical entertainment is under way at this camp. Dennis Kyne is performing for Camp Casey.

12:25 p.m. Deborah Mathews reporting from Pirate Field in Crawford, Texas:

Yellow ribbons are tied around trees, telephone poles, and tent poles throughout this area. Several individual group initiatives are taking place at various sites throughout the Crawford area. American flags are everywhere.

Singing is going on as I stand by a van that says FreeRepublic.com. A lot of people are leading dogs around. A huge American flag is hanging from a type of crane and it has pictures and little signs all over it. It is about seventy-five feet tall.

Many red, white, and blue balloons and banners are around.

A FreeRepublic member commented that the gathering is about protecting the troops in Iraq. Some of the activities of anti-war protestors directly endanger our troops, he said.

Media is out in full force at this site.

It was noted that Camp Qualls is not part of this rally,

which is sponsored by MoveAmericaForward and Free-Republic.

The California caravan has not yet arrived, but the number of individuals here is currently estimated at over 500, and people are constantly streaming in.

Thus far, traffic congestion is not a big problem.

The weather is unbelievably hot. With the high humidity, standing in the sun is nearly unbearable.

About 200 people were at Camp Qualls prior to my moving to Pirate Field. They had been there for a dedication ceremony, according to attendees.

The rally was initially planned for 1 p.m., but with a delay in the California caravan arriving it might be slightly delayed. Musical entertainment is being held on the stage.

12:40 p.m. Deborah Mathews reporting from Pirate Field:

The California caravan has now arrived and the rally is apparently beginning early. Melanie Morgan is onstage saying "this is what's going on, so let's get going." I'll report back shortly.

12:45 p.m. Gene Ellis reporting from Camp Casey II:

There are probably 2,000 people or more in the big tent at Camp Casey II. There is a rally under way on the stage with a man, and now the entire audience, singing "God Bless America." Coordinator Ann Wright spoke for a few minutes earlier. A huge luncheon is set out with people lined up. Another busload of people is driving up right now. Parking is pretty much maxed out now.

Ann Wright is currently speaking again. You can smell barbecue cooking. Programs on stage are continuing during the day. Gatorade and water is being passed out among the crowd.

People just keep piling in. It is very hot.

There is going to be a wedding tomorrow at 4 p.m. at Camp Casey II. The bride says she will find and wear the cleanest T-shirt she's got and the money that would be have been spent on the wedding will go to the Peace House and Cindy Sheehan's group.

1:00 p.m. Deborah Mathews reporting from Pirate Field:

People are literally pouring in at Pirate Field, so the rally has been delayed to accommodate them. I'll report back shortly.

[*The Iconoclast,* Vol. 6, No.35, August 31, 2005.]

1:15 p.m. Gene Ellis reporting from Camp Casey II:

Joan Baez has returned and just led everyone in singing "Amazing Grace" at Camp Casey II. When she finished she said, "Christian right, eat your heart out."

Baez's songs will be interspersed throughout the rally this afternoon. The barbecue is still to follow, as is the continued rally. Various artists from Austin are slated to perform later.

Another busload of people has come in. Several helicopters are flying about.

1:15 p.m. Deborah Mathews reporting from Pirate Field:

There are upwards of a thousand people here now.

A group of three people were walking away from the rally. One woman was carrying a sign tucked into her pants that said, "Liar, liar, pants on fire, George W. Bush, is it burning yet?"

American flags are in hats, red, white, and blue on clothes. People are carrying signs.

The chairs under the tent are full. Barbecue is being sold; a tent is set up for Gold Star Families.

People of all ages and types are here.

One shirt said, "I hate hippies."

One sign says, "We support President Bush. Period."

Someone just sang "a cappella" and is receiving big applause. Now, they are chanting "U.S.A. Support Our Troops." Flags are literally everywhere.

1:17 p.m. Michael Harvey reporting from Camp Casey I:

At Camp Casey I, it is hot, probably 110 degrees. Members on each side of the triangle are yelling at each other, veterans for the war on one side, veterans against the war on the other. They are taunting each other.

The crowd is growing and parking has become a big problem.

At the pro-Bush side of the encampment, a hot-dog stand has been set up.

1:30 p.m. Michael Harvey reporting from Camp Casey I:

At Camp Casey I, the Bush side is chanting "George Bush!" and the anti-war side is finishing their sentence by chanting "War criminal!"

The Bush side is loudly calling out, "Where is your anti-Semitic leader?"

One pro-war sign says, "Cindy and Osama sitting in a tree." Another says "Who's paying you?"

A bunch of cars are passing by honking, as they have been doing constantly today.

Now the Bush side is yelling, "I'm for W."

There are close to 200 people out here now (both sides combined).

Music and barbecue is planned on the Camp Casey side this afternoon.

1:45 p.m. Deborah Mathews reporting from Pirate Field:

There are apparently three Cindy Sheehan supporters out here in the middle of the crowd. Their signs appear to have been torn up and they are being escorted away by law enforcement personnel. (I heard later that these people were lost or confused and ended up at the wrong place—way wrong.)

These people are serious out here.

Someone's yelling, "That's what they want to do, distract us."

People in the crowd roar at any given moment.

Melanie Morgan just screamed out, "This is not Vietnam." The crowd absolutely erupted.

The father of a boy in sniper training in Iraq said he spoke with his son on the phone who said, "Cindy Sheehan shut up. You're getting us killed."

"Cindy go home" is what the crowd is chanting now.

One sign says, "Cindy Sheehan, the bitch in the ditch."

There are now 2,000 plus people out here.

Morgan said, "Let's get this show running, keep it running, because afterwards, we're taking the fight to Cindy."

Someone just yelled, "There go Cindy's pimps, the media."

People are still coming up the road, ten or fifteen at a time.

A fireman whose twin brother was killed in Iraq just delivered a speech. He said that about two weeks short of retirement the brother was killed and "this is a war about good and evil, and we are winning it. My brother died for what he believed in."

Someone is yelling, "Those of you that were spit on, brutalized, had your soul stolen after returning from Vietnam... That is not going to happen again."

There is a huge mob around the stage, and a lot of flatbed trailers filled with everybody from the media to Uncle Sam clones.

There is the policeman who escorted the Cindy Sheehan supporters away.

(Moments later)—I just asked him, "Was there any violence," and he said, "I can't..." (and paused) Then smiled and said "Are you a reporter." I said, "Yes." Then he walked off and said, "Oh, that explains it." I didn't get an answer.

It is intense here. Intense is a mild word.

2:20 p.m. Deborah Mathews reporting from Pirate Field:

Deena Burnett, wife Tom Burnett, Jr. who was on the plane that crashed into a field during 9/11, just spoke, saying, "We have a responsibility to our troops. Our nation stands divided. This war is not about us. We fight for those who can't fight for themselves like my husband did.

"Our soldiers are doing what it takes to keep another

September 11 from happening anywhere in our world.

"Thankfully, our leaders didn't sway with public opinion and not fight. I stand in support of our troops," she continued. "Our troops are promoting a better quality of life for the people in Iraq. I commend them for that and I thank them for their service to America and the world."

The mother of Army CWO Eric Kesterson, said, "My husband and I are not here speaking out. We are speaking up."

A man is now being carried away via ambulance. He was conscious, but his condition is unknown at this time.

People are still arriving in droves. There are probably 3,000-4,000 people here now and still coming.

3:00 p.m. Deborah Mathews reporting from Pirate Field:

The rally is now complete and people are disbursing. People are making their way toward vehicles. Members of Gold Star Families are headed toward Camp Casey I, accompanied by law enforcement, to remove crosses bearing names of their family members that have been planted in the ditch.

4:20 p.m. Deborah Mathews reporting from Pirate Field:

At and around the Yellow Rose, people are milling around watching the goings-on. Right now, there are several hundred there. Some boys about high school age walking in the direction of Pirate Field just yelled, "Cindy, the fucking whore, get out."

It appears there are a lot of spectators around, simply watching history in the making.

A man a block from the Yellow Rose carrying a white cross, yelled out to me, "Be sure you send this to your friends in Iraq." The sign he carried said "Real America won't wimp out." When asked, "What? The photo?" and he said "Yeah, I want them to see it."

Now here's a U-Haul truck beside the road that says, "A mother's loss, a nation's pain."

The railroad crossing bars have been going off, up and then down, up and then down, but no train.

People are pulling on a rope that has been tied to the gong on the Liberty Bell at the Yellow Rose. This is happening frequently.

This is certainly not what I expected, not this level of passion and intensity on both sides.

4:20 p.m. Gene Ellis reporting from Camp Casey II:

Joan Baez sang about four times this afternoon, a couple of the songs being "Joe Hill" and "The Night They Drove Old Dixie Down."

Cindy Sheehan spoke at the rally and at a press conference just after that.

Sheehan said that before she came down here, someone told her, "You should go down in a pasture near Bush's ranch and thousands of people would come and you ought to call it Turdstock, so let's call it Turdstock."

She said that one question in her mind when she first arrived in Crawford was: "When will America care?" Now, she says, she knows that America cares.

Sheehan talked about her plans to take her message to the communities, that it is a grassroots movement that's growing and growing. She said, "I couldn't stop it now if I wanted to. It's got a life of its own. We'll take it to the cities, then the House and the Senate." She reiterated that the insurgency is fueled by our presence. She says she thinks it will stop if we leave.

The serving of barbecue has not yet started. The arrival of persons to have crosses removed has not happened.

There are still thousands here. Few, if any, are leaving. People keep arriving.

DAY TWENTY-THREE
Sunday, August 28, 2005

LIGHTNING STRIKES!

The Iconoclast had been posting the text updates first, as events occurred, then after processing photographs, posting them, since it takes time to choose which to use, resize the choices, then write the captions.

Unfortunately, on Saturday night, around 7 p.m., a lightning storm resulted in a loss of internet power, shutting down the paper's capability of uploading new material.

The system did not function properly until Sunday afternoon. Since the newspaper was deep into production of the print edition, and behind at that, there were no Sunday postings, but the stories derived from Sunday's coverage were posted very late. In other matters on Sunday, a wedding was held during the early afternoon. Former presidential candidate Reverend Al Sharpton visited Camp Casey II, Sunday morning, as did Ben Boothe.

Musical entertainment took place during the day.

Here are those stories:

BATTLEGROUND CRAWFORD
Dueling Movements Ignite Upon Return of Cindy Sheehan
Crawford Bulges at the Seams
By W. Leon Smith, Editor-in-Chief

[Cindy Sheehan speaking during the protest rally in Crawford, TX.]

CRAWFORD—Approximately 7,000 demonstrators temporarily inhabited Crawford Saturday as two pro-American factions gathered in a variety of venues to express support for troops in Iraq.

The difference, however, was how the groups defined "support."

What sparked the Saturday invasion was a journey to Crawford by Cindy Sheehan on August 6. The mother of a slain soldier in the Iraq war took exception to remarks made by President Bush regarding the "noble cause" for which the soldiers have been fighting. She was seeking a personal conversation with the President in order to obtain a truthful explanation.

The President, however, has declined Sheehan's initiative. She, therefore, has been camping between Crawford and the Bush ranch, resolving to meet with the head of state while he takes his annual extended vacation.

Sheehan was called away to Los Angeles about midway through her vigil after her mother suffered a stroke, but Sheehan returned on Wednesday.

What began as Camp Casey, named after her son, has in the meantime expanded into two camps, Camp Casey I, at the original site in a ditch, and Camp Casey II, nearer the Bush ranch on private property donated by a local landowner. Assisting Sheehan have been organizations and individuals supporting her cause and an end to the war in Iraq.

As the international news media zeroed-in on the story of a mother seeking answers for her son's death, an opposition camp was established adjacent to Camp Casey I. Dubbed "Camp Reality," it has consisted of pro-war demonstrators who support the President's determination to "stay the course" with the war.

The Yellow Rose gift shop in downtown Crawford hosted the creation of yet another pro-Bush camp, Camp Qualls, named after another soldier who died in Iraq. It is here that pro-Bush supporters have met to plan strategies. An additional camp was established near Crawford, again in support of Bush, called Camp George.

Saturday's uprising, in 101-plus-degree, sweltering weather, consisted of pro-Bush advocates venturing to the 700-population community, staging a patriotic demonstration in an attempt to squash protestors against the war.

On the parking lot of Crawford High School's Pirate Field, Howard Kaloogian, founder of Move America Forward, said that Sheehan's anti-war protest feeds the Iraq insurgency. "The terrorists that are watching Cindy Sheehan's protest believe that this is something that might topple the current administration," he said.

A minor disruption occurred at the "You Don't Speak for Me, Cindy!" rally when Ken Robinson of Richardson appeared carrying a sign that read "How to wreck your family in thirty days by 'bitch in the ditch' Cindy Sheehan."

When an event organizer with FreeRepublic.com approached Robinson to object to the sign, voices were raised and Robinson was escorted in handcuffs away from the rally by a Woodway police officer.

Someone in the crowd yelled as the press filmed the encounter, "There go Cindy's pimps, the media."

Throughout the day on Saturday, busloads of Sheehan supporters numbering in the thousands arrived at Camp Casey II where entertainment and speeches highlighted their movement.

During the afternoon, *The Iconoclast* stationed reporters at Pirate Field parking lot, where the pro-Bush rally was held, and later at Camp Qualls. Reporters were also stationed at the segment of road inhabited by Camp Casey I and Camp Reality, and at Camp Casey II, to file reports for www.iconoclast-texas.com and the afternoon broadcast of the Brad Show via raw radio, which has been broadcasting events related to Cindy Sheehan's since August 15.

The rally near Pirate Field started later than the announced 1 p.m. kickoff time due to the continuous arrival of anti-Sheehan demonstrators, as traffic congestion in Crawford boiled.

The Iconoclast's Deborah Mathews described the scene this way:

Individuals arriving at Camp Casey I and Camp Reality were told by law enforcement personnel to choose a side and stay on that side.

Several busloads of anti-war demonstrators journeyed to Camp Casey II during the day, where a large tent-like pavilion had been set up for about a week. An estimated 3,000 people ventured to this camp during the day, most staying to hear speeches and music.

Among the entertainers was folk singer Joan Baez, who kicked off the noon hour with "Amazing Grace," and later sang "The Night They Drove Old Dixie Down." Barbecue was being cooked for a massive feed later in the day.

Also appearing on stage was American Indian activist and performer Russell Means, who expounded upon the importance of women in society. He praised Sheehan for her stand against war.

Other speakers included veterans who are members of organizations that oppose the Iraq war.

When Sheehan took the stage, she talked about her plans to take her message "to the communities," describing the mission as a "grass-roots movement that's growing and growing." She said, "I couldn't stop it now if I wanted to. It's got a life of its own. We'll take it to the cities, then the House and the Senate."

Russell Means Visits Camp Casey
Means Says He Understands Power Of Women
By Gene Ellis, *Iconoclast* Reporter

[American Indian activist Russell Means speaking at Camp Casey II.]

CAMP CASEY II—Russell Means' appearance on the stage at Camp Casey II in Crawford yesterday was a surprise to many. For background on this famous Indian (who eschews the government term "Native American"), see brief additional biographical information at the end of this story.

Means, a long-time activist, arrived in central Texas to support the efforts of Cindy Sheehan and her Iraq war protestors. He well understands the power of women. He spoke, both on stage and in a later interview with *The Iconoclast*, of the matriarchal society of the American Indian.

Motherhood in America has an inkling of the meaning of this, Means mused, but the Indians live it.

He explained that in a family, the mother is the only member who cannot be replaced. Women live longer than men, can stand more pain, have more endurance, he said. At about this point, Means introduced his wife, Pearl, and received a hug from Joan Baez, who was sitting on the floor of the stage with Cindy Sheehan, listening to Means' remarks.

Means said that America has a patriarchal society where men rule alone and in fear of the unknown because they are alone. Matriarchy, he pointed out, is not fear-based. In a matriarchal society, each sex is celebrated for its strengths, and there is local control, male/female balance.

During the later interview with *The Iconoclast*, Means made a point of saying that he is sincere about women taking control of their power, providing a balanced and positive culture. The Blue and Gold Star mothers have an innate understanding of matriarchy, according to Means, even though, as members of a patriarchal society, they have been brainwashed for many years.

In a matriarchal society, all must be responsible.

"If the government of this country imposes so many rules, we feel no responsibility for ourselves, and we become careless," said Means. To illustrate his point, he used the example of the lack of traffic rules in Italy. Because there are no rules, each person must take it upon him or herself to be responsible, not to be careless, to ensure his or her own safety.

When asked to speak about military recruiters targeting low-income youths, including Indians, Means said that it follows the history of a patriarchal society that the poor kids are to be the cannon fodder. Even after the Civil War, when Americans wouldn't join the military, European immigrants were pulled off boats and forced to do two years of subscripted service to obtain citizenship. The poor are always a target for military induction, Means concluded.

Means reiterated that if men rule alone in their citadels of power, they are fearful.

A Libertarian, Means paraphrased George Washington, "Government is force, nothing more, nothing less."

Means added to this his own thoughts, "This government is evil. How can patriots support a President over the Constitution? That is treason. The purpose of the First Amendment is to encourage dissent. Without dissent, it is impossible to live free."

His comments were reminiscent of Margaret Mead's quote that has graced the back of many a T-shirt in Crawford over the last two weeks. It reads, "Never doubt that a small group of thoughtful, committed citizens can change the world; indeed, it is the only thing that ever has."

The Los Angeles Times has described Russell Means as the most famous American Indian since Sitting Bull and Crazy Horse.

Means is a life-long indigenous rights/constitutional rights activist, actor, artist, and author. His best selling autobiography *Where White Men Fear to Tread* is currently on its eighth printing. He has a doctorate in Indian Studies, and is also a practicing attorney on the Sioux Indian Reservation in South Dakota.

For more than thirty years, Means has remained active with the American Indian Movement and has traveled and lectured extensively throughout the world while working for over twelve years with the United Nations.

Means became the first national director of the American Indian Movement (AIM). He is known for helping lead his people to stand against the United States government at the Siege of Wounded Knee in 1973.

His vision is for indigenous people to be free—free to be human, free to travel, free to shop, free to trade where they choose, free to choose their own teachers—free to follow the religion of their fathers, free to talk, think and act for themselves, and then, says Means, they will obey every law or submit to the penalty.

About the Siege at Wounded Knee, he wrote, "Our aim at Wounded Knee was to force the U.S. government to live up to its own laws. From that, one can draw the real lesson of our stand there: It is the duty of every responsible American to ensure that their government upholds the spirit and the laws of the United States Constitution. After all, what freedom really means is that you are free to be responsible."

Martin Sheen Visits Camp Casey
West Wing Actor Sheen Pays Visit to Camp Casey II
By Michael Harvey, *Iconoclast* Reporter

CRAWFORD—Cindy Sheehan and Camp Casey received a huge boost Sunday, both in support and in morale. Actor Martin Sheen came to visit. It had been rumored for some time that Sheen might make an appearance, and today, the rumor came to fruition.

Sheen arrived around 5:30 p.m. with very little fanfare, and was greeted warmly by the crowd. Judging by the hugs and kisses, it was obvious that he and some of the Camp Casey clan already knew each other. After a five-minute photo session, Sheen retreated to the trailer that had been set up for Cindy Sheehan, where he was introduced to some family members of fallen soldiers.

[Actor/activist Martin Sheen viewing the memorial crosses during his visit to Camp Casey.]

It was described as a very passionate time that included many hugs, kisses, smiles, and even a few tears. Sheen was warm and friendly, and eagerly had his photo taken with many people. The time that Sheen spent near the trailer was low-key, intimate, and personal.

After some singing and talking on the stage, it was time for Sheen and Sheehan. Joining the two on stage were Iraqi veterans and family members of those who had fallen in Iraq. Sheen began his speech with a brief history of vigils.

"It is an Irish tradition. When a person had a disagreement with a landlord, for example, that person would stand vigil outside that landlord's home until he came out to talk with them," he said. "You all know what I do for a living, but this is what I do to stay alive."

The crowd roared after hearing that.

Sheen continued to speak for a few minutes, and was followed by Sheehan, who spoke of her son as a devoted Catholic. Everyone who knew Casey was aware of his strong faith. She described how, when his body was brought home to America, eleven Catholic Rosaries had been placed with him by his fellow soldiers. That gave her some peace, she said.

During Sheehan's speaking, Sheen spent more time greeting soldiers and the families of soldiers.

He again was willing to shake hands, give hugs, pose for photos, and sign autographs for anyone who asked.

Sheen then rejoined Sheehan on stage, and along with about ten other people, began a Rosary vigil. After each prayer of the Rosary that Sheen said, Sheehan called out the name of a fallen soldier. Many tears were shed during this vigil, which lasted nearly an hour.

Sheehan called out the names of approximately fifty fallen soldiers. Following the vigil was a time for song, including "Amazing Grace." Fittingly, during the line "Bright shining as the sun," a yellow-orange sunset shone through the tent and onto the stage. Until that moment, the sun had been blocked all day by an overcast sky.

After the singing concluded, Sheehan and Sheen each spoke to the crowd briefly before heading to the field of crosses erected at Camp Casey II. Along the way, the two posed for pictures with members of Iraq Veterans Against the War. They then moved to the middle of the field that contained crosses, flags, and flowers, and joined by approximately twenty friends, observed a moment of silence. This moment of silence preceded the playing of "Taps" by Lance Corporal Jeff Key and the singing of "God Bless America."

Sheehan and Sheen then knelt in front of Casey Sheehan's cross and said a prayer together. Cindy wept, and after hugging Sheen goodbye, retreated to her trailer. The actor made one last round of good-byes, again stopping to hug and thank as many people as possible.

Sheen's visit to Camp Casey II was described by many as powerful and meaningful. It was a stirring way to begin the final few days of the protest and vigil near Crawford.

DAY TWENTY-FOUR
Monday, August 29, 2005

12:00 p.m. Gene Ellis reporting:

It has been a slow morning. Some of the camps broke up last night due to high winds, so the population has decreased a bit.

There will be a candlelight vigil at Camp I tonight. There will be dinner honoring volunteers at Camp II tomorrow.

DAY TWENTY-FIVE
Tuesday, August 30, 2005

11:30 a.m. Gene Ellis reporting:

As some people are breaking up camp, many leftover supplies are starting to go to relief efforts in New Orleans in the wake of Hurricane Katrina.

This morning, at the 10:30 a.m. press conference at Camp Casey II, details of the bus tour were announced. It will leave at 11:30 a.m. Wednesday.

Today, a ceremony was held to remove first the flowers, then the flags, then the crosses from Arlington West, the area in front of Camp Casey II, which is under way now.

About 100 or so people are at Camp Casey II, and a few remain at Camp Casey I and Camp Reality (the pro-Bush camp across the triangle from Camp Casey I).

It is hot here, not horrendous yet. Food serving is about to begin.

7:00 p.m. Gene Ellis reporting:

A dinner was held tonight at Camp Casey II to thank the volunteers. Dismantling of both camps is under way. Many unused supplies, tarps, and tents will go to the New Orleans area to assist in the aftermath of Hurricane Katrina. These items will be transported by veterans.

Buses will leave Wednesday from Camp Casey II at approximately 10:30 a.m. Volunteers are being asked to remain in the area through Thursday or Friday until the land is left as it was.

There were rumors around camp that were later confirmed to be true: Bush's senior political advisor and deputy chief of staff Karl Rove paid a visit Tuesday night to Camp Reality, across the road from Camp Casey I. He reportedly visited with about half-a-dozen pro-Bush activists.

This occurred when most of the Sheehan supporters were away from that area, enjoying the final thank-you dinner at Camp Casey II.

DAY TWENTY-SIX
Wednesday, August 31, 2005

2:00 p.m. Gene Ellis reporting:
FINAL CRAWFORD UPDATE

Buses were being packed all morning for departing Cindy Sheehan supporters and relief materials for the New Orleans area at Camp Casey I.

Sheehan held a press conference and told the remaining supporters that she was very grateful for all their help during these days at Crawford. She said, "I never thought when I started here that I would be sad to leave, but I am. We outstayed President Bush."

Sheehan reiterated that the movement would not end until the soldiers came home, that on September 24 in Washington, D.C. "We must tell the President that we have had enough and hold him accountable for the death and destruction he has caused."

Sheehan planned to depart on the same veterans' bus on which she arrived, but will leave the tour at some point and rejoin the buses in about a week.

Sheehan mentioned that she found it difficult to believe that President Bush said yesterday, that we should protect the oil fields from terrorists. She asked, "How many of you are willing to sacrifice one of your children to be able to pay over $3 a gallon for gas?"

"It was for oil after all," she added, "and that's not a good enough reason."

"We need to spend our money on renewable energy sources so no one else has to die. There was no noble cause," she said.

Sheehan urged people to consult her website, bring-themhomenow.org, and to pressure their elected officials to end the war.

The buses departed Camp Casey I at approximately 11 a.m. and headed to the Peace House. A light luncheon was served while people said their goodbyes. The four RVs were prepared with banners and slogans. Some supporters sang and danced, and cheers accompanied the departing vans and the veterans' bus as they left on their three-week tour.

The cleanup continues at the two camps.

REPORTER PERSPECTIVES

Impressions by reporters covering the twenty-six day vigil near Crawford, Texas

DEBORAH MATHEWS:

Whether remembered as the "bitch in the ditch" or the era's "moral icon," the name of Cindy Sheehan is forever part of history. Good, bad, or somewhere in between, the world knows of her.

What may not be as easily understood is the fact that no matter what position one had, Cindy Sheehan awoke the world. Passion was ignited through the exchange of strong opinion and moral perspectives.

Now, in the wake of her endeavor, opinion is still strong and a once slumbering people are again taking part in the world.

No one was prepared for the onslaught that would become *The Vigil*—I certainly wasn't. The grueling fifteen-hour days with copy deadlines, the constant news coverage in the 100+ degree heat, and the skipped meals all fall away when I think of the depths of human nature I was fortunate to witness during my time with Cindy Sheehan.

From people full of kindness, compassion, and an indescribable intensity, to those filled with true cruelty and hatred, all were part of the wave of humanity that filled this pocket of time.

People were either for or against her. There wasn't any gray area. Apathy was just not possible.

Personally torn between my private opinions and duties as a journalist, this was an extremely difficult situation for me, and it only intensified as the number of people involved grew.

Whether at Pirate Field or Camp Casey, I had to constantly remind myself that I was a reporter, not a supporter. I struggled to remember that the heated discussions held in the office had no place in Crawford. I really had to remember why I was putting myself through all of this when I would be either hugged or shoved, depending on where I stood at the time.

I was also unprepared for the amount of international interest that this story drew. When the BBC of Scotland called, or the calls from Italy and England came in on my personal cell phone, I had to pause and re-evaluate my involvement. Should I do these interviews? Why do they care? With each new day I had to be reminded that this was something of worth, and each new day came with its own obstacles.

There came a point when I was no longer unsure. I became completely determined to tell the world how life was in Crawford.

That turning point came during a live interview on MSNBC. The anchor asked questions of happenings in Crawford and the overall conditions. When she asked about how Larry Mattlage "fired his gun at Camp Casey supporters," something snapped in me. Knowing that he had not fired at anyone, having been only feet from him when the shooting began, I was infuriated to hear that reports had depicted him as some hillbilly farmer with a vengeance. Sure, he was angry. Sure, he fired his gun; but he did not fire at anyone or anything. That was the first time I really got angry and wanted to share an editorial opinion.

My background allows me a clear insight into life in the country, and that life doesn't normally include traffic jams and Porta-Potties.

When temperatures are over 100 degrees, animals have to be watered. If I had dry-lotted cattle a five-minute drive away that had to be watered, but had spend forty-five minutes picking my way through cars, people, pets, I would be tempted to strongly remind people that they were in my backyard, too. Many people's livelihood depends on those cattle. At times this seemed to go unnoticed, intentionally or not. I wondered: Was a rural community of 702 people the place to make such a stand?

One thing that I had no trouble remembering was that these "country people" (and I say that with the deepest respect, being pure country myself) have rights, too. The First Amendment applies to Crawford residents as well as those opposed to Cindy Sheehan and her cause.

As hard as I tried not to have an opinion, when it came to the scale of the disruption to the residents of Crawford, Texas, it was impossible.

The first time I saw a school bus full of children pass through the protest zone, I thought of my own kids. Would I want them anywhere near here? No.

I don't want to offend or pass judgment, but simply say: There were people coming and going in Crawford who made me uncomfortable. There were more than a few instances that I actually feared I was in the wrong place at the wrong time.

Was I losing more than I was gaining by helping to "write" history? And what were the larger social implications?

Yes, simply. I may not have agreed with much of it, but I still could not deny the impact of this phenomenon.

I responded to anyone requesting an interview of me in the same way. I told them that I would be happy to help, but that I would not give opinion, so not to ask.

As I recount the events in Crawford now, it's impossible not to remember how I felt when it was reported that Cindy got her hair cut. I didn't care that Cindy got a haircut—I didn't have time to get my own hair done.

It's impossible not to recall my genuine disgust—and a bit of real fear—when an outside police officer treated me as though I carried the plague, and all the while people were screaming, "Cindy's pimps, the damn media."

I will not deny that I had to hide behind some trees at Pirate Field and dry tears from my face as I witnessed the abounding pride and emotion of something I considered to be the most heartfelt patriotism I would ever experience.

I remember our nation's—no, the world's—mourning in the days following 9/11. I wanted to throw my arms around the mothers and fathers at Pirate Field who had buried their children, and still cried: "One nation, under God!"

At the same time, I remembered the mourning of my own mother and father many years ago as they buried my brother, and I wanted to comfort Cindy and say: "What's happening is right and good. Nothing makes the death of a child okay."

Another personal memory of a time past came to me and helped to remind me why I was there: family history.

In an attempt to comfort me after the death of my brother, my grandfather told me of the loss of his own brother in WWII, on the beach of Normandy. He spoke of the sorrow of the loss, but also of the result of a life given to a cause greater than one. He showed me newspaper clippings that read, "… first Canadian County boy returns home on the train… died in the cause of this great nation… honor him for his sacrifice…" He also told me of a star that hung on the wall of the county courthouse with my great uncle's name on it. Though I did feel a surge of pride, I was more affected by the memory. He would be remembered throughout history not only for his sacrifice, but also because that sacrifice was recorded and remembered.

Not intending to compare Cindy Sheehan to a fallen soldier, I am compelled to give her due credit for invoking passion in a world mired in its complexities. As my father so often said, "There is right and there is wrong. There is no gray. It is black or it is white." Regardless of which side of Prairie Chapel Road people chose to stand during this historic event, they did stand. There was no one in the middle.

A lifetime can be spent wondering "what if." I will always wonder if my displeasure at being involved showed in my reporting. If it did, I am truly regretful. Something I will never wonder about is how it feels to be active in the world.

Cindy Sheehan is just a person. As time moves on and her name is repeated, whether with a sneer or in revered tones, her name will punctuate history, and will remind us of what it is to be American. If she accomplished nothing else, Cindy Sheehan reminded us that we have an opinion and that in our great country, we have also been given the right to share it. Right or wrong, she took her stand in Crawford and I took mine and reported it to the world.

GENE ELLIS SILLS, Ed.D.:

In a way, it was reminiscent of summer camp. And I mean no disrespect. But this was a summer camp for adults, and for adults with serious convictions, a very grave message and grown-up concerns. When folks in Crawford discovered I had written a mostly humorous column before diving headlong into my middle-aged stint as a cub reporter, a few asked if I had found much humor there.

The truth is, not really. I reported news and interviewed people from both sides of the issue. My eyes often welled up on either side of the triangle dividing Camp Casey I from the smaller band of polite, peaceful Bush supporters. I cried at the Peace House, at Camp Qualls, at Camp Casey II. It was hard for me personally to get past the fact that I was speaking with parents, friends, and family members who had lost loved ones. At that level, it didn't much matter if their sentiments were pro- or anti-war. I wept with them all. Openly. I have my own opinions, which I often keep to myself, non-confrontational little person that I am.

Although there were light moments, music, smiles, rallying and celebrating, it wasn't a humorous situation. On that last Saturday, when "unknown quantities" arrived on buses to support both sides, it could have been very dangerous. Thankfully, it was not, due in great degree to peacekeeping workshops on both sides and the gargantuan support of local law enforcement. With a few exceptions (when tempers flared or agitators tried to make trouble), most everyone did themselves proud.

People came to little Crawford, Texas, from all over the country over the last couple of weeks, and the most prevalent reason given by the Sheehan supporters was: "I felt I had to come." They were compelled. A lot likened the strong pull they felt to that showcased in the movie, *Close Encounters of the Third Kind.* These are definitely people with passion. Many of them had been checking updates on *The Iconoclast* website, and others then saw coverage by the mainstream media. They saw what was going on, and there was no choice for them. They took vacations. They took leaves of absence. They kissed friends and family goodbye, and arrived in droves from every part of this country and even beyond.

I have no doubt that many pro-Bush/pro-war supporters also felt the same compulsion, but I didn't hear that reason given as much when speaking to them. About fifty percent of those polled at the football stadium on "the last Saturday" said they had come in response to an e-mail urging them to attend the pro-Bush rally in Crawford. It was from the National Republican Party. They arrived on buses mainly, rallied, then left, most on the same day.

Camp Qualls, (another pro-Bush venue adjacent to

the Yellow Rose, a gift shop in Crawford), was host to a usually small but steady stream of visitors during the last week or so of August. Then there was that hardy band of more independent pro-Bush supporters on the "other side of the triangle" from Camp Casey I. They wanted to show support for the troops and the President.

Like summer camp, people on both sides forged friendships and alliances (although not usually with those on the opposing side) due to common interests. Several old friends were reunited. Romance even blossomed, and in at least one case, sadly, a marriage was broken, perhaps irreconcilably, over a very strong difference of opinion. These folks camped together and worked together, if not in the trenches, then certainly in the ditches (and fields), for over two weeks in terribly hot, oppressive Texas summer weather.

Bonding occurred, networking abounded. Business cards were exchanged. If it was the sixties, it was the sixties with a twist. Cell phones rang, and bloggers sat before computer screens out in the middle of Nowhere, Texas. Some on each side might have brought along their own agendas, but that was the exception rather than the rule, and those were obvious.

Happily, there were a few instances of people from different sides of the issue coming together to shake hands, praying together, crying together over their losses. They agreed to disagree, but in peace, and with respect.

To me, those encounters were some of the high points, often missed by others or overlooked, certainly by the mainstream media. I know I would never have spoiled that meeting of Gold Star parents with a camera flash, not for all the notoriety in the world. Not every moment should be recorded on tape.

Everyone, with the notable exception of the Reverend Al Sharpton and his driver, praised the efforts of the law enforcement officials. (The driver was arrested for speeding, among other things, as he raced between Camp Casey II and the Waco airport after the interfaith prayer service on "the last Sunday"). The men and women of the various law enforcement teams worked tirelessly to assure the safety of all present.

Everyone wanted to be Sid and John's new best friend. If you were there, you know who they were. They are member of the Sheriff's Department, and they were a constant presence. Most people who followed the events in Crawford in the news will have only an inkling as to the dedication of the various law enforcement officials. They assured the safety of the public in Crawford during these last few weeks. These officers worked long, hot hours, and showed courtesy and consideration to each of the sides. During the very few times it was necessary, they defused situations swiftly, professionally, and without undue force.

As Peter Johnson of the SCLC (who marched with the Reverend Martin Luther King, Jr.) told me, and I agreed: "It wasn't this way in the sixties." How well I remember. I also remember Kent State. This powder keg had that potential. Instead, respect was earned on both sides (excepting a few troublemakers), and importantly too, in the middle, where the law enforcement officials used their cars to provide a physical barrier if necessary.

Officers from the Sheriff's Department, the Texas Highway Patrol, and the Crawford Police Department never, to my knowledge, voiced their own viewpoints with regards to the Big Question.

As Lieutenant Sid Franklin told me, "I will do my best to do my duty to protect them all." And he did.

They all did. Sheriff's deputies even became involved as go-betweens on Saturday when the population of little Crawford, Texas swelled by the thousands and tempers flared. When families of fallen soldiers arrived at Camp Casey I and asked to have names removed from the display of crosses (which had actually been brought from California, a traveling exhibition), Lieutenant Franklin assured them it would be taken care of. This wasn't his job. But there was no contact allowed that day between the two opposing sides. Franklin saw a need and he rose to meet it. He was the professional, compassionate middleman, doing a job that had to be done, respecting the wishes of grieving families.

Like summer camp, when it was all over, many were sad to leave their new friends and that sense of camaraderie and empowerment, sad to leave a place where small voices had joined together to grow large. They had found, in the oppressively hot, central Texas summer, a platform (in a pasture) where, on either side of the question, their feelings about the war and about our President could be voiced without fear.

There were plenty of hugs at Camp Casey I and the Peace House yesterday. Cindy Sheehan herself said: "I never thought when I started here that I would be sad to leave, but I am."

MICHAEL HARVEY:

My involvement began as just an errand. I was to take one of our reporters some extra batteries and an extra memory card for her camera. By the end, I was knee deep in one of the largest events central Texas and the nation had seen in decades.

In the hot August sun, in the Heart of Texas, Cindy Sheehan made history. Camp Casey, named after her fallen son, was an event that will be remembered for generations to come. A lone woman went into the President's backyard and dared to challenge him.

Not being a reporter by trade, I was not prepared for what I would experience. In fact, I was quite overwhelmed. I was shoulder to shoulder with the "Big Boys" in the media—CNN, MSNBC, and Fox News, to name a few. After a while, I came to realize that I *was* one of the "Big Boys."

Almost everyone had heard of *The Lone Star Iconoclast*, and every one of them showered us with praises.

If I were to sum up the event in one word, it would have to be "intense."

There was intense emotion. What else could be expected from a mother who had lost her son in Iraq and was surrounded by Iraq veterans and families of other fallen soldiers? Some people were yelling and screaming, some were singing and dancing, some were crying.

There was intense reaction. The media was constantly following Sheehan around, sticking their cameras and tape recorders in her face. Many of those same people, who had just leached onto Sheehan to get their photos and sound-bites, would walk away mumbling words of ridicule.

Then there were the pro-Bush/pro-war/anti-Cindy protesters who showed up mid-way through the event. Consisting of both adults and children, they would curse and demean Cindy and her supporters.

There were intense conditions. The Camp Casey crowd had to sleep in tents on the side of the road and had limited access to showers and Porta-Potties. All of this was compounded by weather conditions. There was nonstop rain for three days, and then there was the Texas summer. It was *hot*, exceeding 100 degrees almost every day.

There were intense crowds. During the week, there were usually a few hundred people at Camp Casey, but on the weekends, with the Camp Casey support and opposition flooding in, the numbers swelled into the thousands. On one weekend, the population of Crawford, Texas skyrocketed from 702 to roughly 7,000.

This was an event that awoke strong feelings within many Americans. The Camp Casey vigil in Crawford, Texas will be remembered in history alongside the Civil Rights marches of the 1960s and the Vietnam War protests of the 1970s.

ABOUT
THE ICONOCLAST

The Lone Star Iconoclast was founded in December 2000, just after the 2000 presidential election but prior to the Supreme Court decision that declared Republican George W. Bush the winner over Democrat Al Gore.

Since 1979, W. Leon Smith had published, along with his father, James W. Smith, a nearby newspaper, *The Clifton Record*, which was founded in 1895 by W. C. O'Bryan, the grandfather of famed pianist Van Cliburn. The Smiths' corporation under which *The Record* operated was Progressive Media Communications, Inc., with each of the two men owning half the stock.

During much of this partnership, the older Smith had been in charge of the advertising department while the younger Smith was in charge of editorial content.

In the late 1990s, James Smith gradually retired from active duty with the newspaper and instead became more of an occasional advisor, a publisher emeritus.

In early December 2000, *The Record* had just endorsed Bush for President, with the feeling that Bush would be a "uniter, not a divider," but it was not a boisterous recommendation.

Upon Bush's purchase of a ranch near Crawford, W. Leon Smith, who had considered starting a newspaper in Crawford several times previously but had been reluctant to do so because of the limited commercial possibilities inside the community, decided to give it another look. He thought that with the inclusion of a former governor to the area, the business climate might improve, but it would still be a gamble.

Several years prior to this, the younger Smith had created a separate corporation, Smith Media, Inc., of which he owned all the stock. Smith Media originated when he sought a construction permit to build a radio station in the area.

Although the radio station deal fell through, the corporation remained. It was under Smith Media that *The Lone Star Iconoclast* was launched.

Smith had long envisioned a multi-edition weekly newspaper consisting of similar opinion/editorial content in several cities, but with different local content pertaining to the diverse locales. He wanted a newspaper that carried a flag that could be used in more than one location, and he wanted a name that would capture the imagination.

Aware that William Cowper Brann had published a controversial newspaper called *Brann's Iconoclast* near Crawford in the late 1890s, Smith chose *Iconoclast* as the name. He had hoped to start with a Crawford edition and perhaps, after it grew, expand to included editions in Dallas, Austin, Houston, El Paso, and perhaps on the Gulf Coast. But Crawford would be first.

With the assistance of a friend, Don M. Fisher, who headed the journalism department at McLennan Community College in Waco, the plan was thoroughly hatched. The pair hoped that perhaps the newspaper would also provide some real-life training for students at the college.

Initially, the newspaper was well received in Crawford. *The Iconoclast* became a charter member of the local chamber of commerce, and coverage of local events, such as school, sports, local activities, community events, and general news inked most of the pages. *The Iconoclast* did maintain an active editorial page, with hard-hitting editorials and columns. Political coverage was abundant, especially when organized activists came to Crawford.

Protests and rallies were regular entries on national calendars, with Crawford as the destination.

Things changed on September 29, 2004.

The Lone Star Iconoclast published a biting editorial endorsing John Kerry for President.

Smith, Fisher, and a young man who had been a reporter for *The Iconoclast* for about two years, Nathan Diebenow, co-wrote the editorial "Kerry Will Restore American Dignity."

About a month prior to that, Smith penned the first draft of the editorial. It was then passed around among the three to be worked on between regular duties, so that each writer could include his own perspectives about how the editorial should be worded and what points should be emphasized.

At the time, political commercials on television were abundant, but, in the view of the editors, the commercials did not focus on issues that would have a long-standing impact on the general population. The campaigns were being trivialized. Therefore, these previously neglected issues became a focal point of the editorial. Also emphasized were the war in Iraq, no-bid contracts, the aftermath of September 11, 2001, and the national debt.

After the finishing touches went onto the editorial and just prior to publication, Don Fisher told Smith, "Do you realize that you could be risking everything with this editorial?"

Smith's reply was, "It's just an editorial, and it's what we believe."

The decision had been made to publish the editorial in September and *The Iconoclast*'s last edition for the month was upon them. This particular edition of the newspaper carried a special supplement in promotion of Crawford's big annual festival, Tonkawa Traditions, which would be held later that week. President Bush was making a surprise visit to his ranch near Crawford to practice for his first presidential debate with John Kerry, so the national press corps was in tow.

After the newspaper hit the streets on Tuesday morning, the 28th, all hell broke loose.

The telephone lines at the Clifton office were jammed with readers canceling their subscriptions to *The Iconoclast*, angry callers were cursing at newspaper staff members then slamming down their phone receivers, businesses were canceling advertisements, and members of the national news media were calling for interviews. Anonymous threats were made on the publisher and an area boycott of the newspaper was started, extending not only to the newspaper company itself, but to anyone who dared to advertise in the newspaper. "Anyone who places an ad in *The Lone Star Iconoclast* will be run out of business," one e-mail said.

Even the neighboring *Clifton Record* lost some long-time subscribers and a few advertisers canceled their bookings, promising to never again have anything to do with that newspaper.

Smith also owned the historic CLIFTEX Theatre. He had purchased the theatre about three years before to keep it open for the youth of the community. It had been a break-even proposition financially, but began to lose money. Some patrons decided that it too should be the subject of a boycott because of the editorial.

Local Republicans began harassing Smith, calling for him to be ousted from his second term as mayor of the City of Clifton. Aldermen on the council refused to consider the requests. Ironically, Smith was elected to a third term a few months later, as the lone candidate for the chief executive seat for the city.

To top it off, former "friends" gave Smith the cold shoulder and strangers he happened to meet on the street administered outright tongue-lashings.

In this regard, Smith found himself in a similar situation as Brann, but minus the shootout on the streets of Waco that claimed Brann's life and ended *Brann's Iconoclast* just over a hundred years ago.

In the days following publication of the editorial, reporters who had nothing to do with the editorial were harassed when they attempted to cover events in Crawford.

Soon after the editorial was posted, the bandwidth on *The Iconoclast* website was maxed out, and there were many times that visitors to the site could not gain access. Blogs began carrying the editorial, and requests from other newspapers to reprint the editorial came in from across the country. Eventually, millions of people read the editorial throughout the world, this perhaps becoming the most-read single editorial of the year.

As days passed, more and more people began to subscribe to *The Iconoclast*, from coast to coast and beyond. New subscriptions replaced those lost and actually overcame that number three-fold.

In all, Smith granted about fifty interviews with newspaper/television/radio reporters from foreign countries, hundreds from media in the United States, and even appeared on the front page of *The New York Times*.

At the request of new supporters of *The Iconoclast*, Smith traveled from coast to coast to speak on the importance of a free press. He wrote an article for the *British Journalism Review* entitled "When Principles Stampede the Herd," about the importance of journalists to forever seek the truth and stand on principle.

Smith received over 10,000 e-mails from throughout the world, about ninety percent of which were positive regarding the editorial. Some, however, were vicious and threatening. He also received about 2,000 letters by mail, and hundreds of phone calls.

The aftermath of the editorial saw the immediate dissolution of the local news network that the newspaper had carefully crafted upon beginning its coverage of Crawford. Teachers would not allow students' photos to appear in the newspaper, news sources for local events dried up, and some businessmen even claimed that *The Iconoclast* was never a part of Crawford, although this was not the case prior to publication of the editorial.

By November, the editors of *The Iconoclast* were facing an identity crisis. The direction, even survival, of the newspaper was in question.

Because of its new-found national circulation and the difficulty in achieving cooperation in Crawford regarding local coverage, *The Iconoclast* went in a different direction. Smith altered the broadsheet format of the newspaper into a tabloid to gain additional independent pages for better organization of the layout. He reduced Crawford community coverage and replaced it with news of national or statewide interest, largely focusing on important stories that the mainstream media might have overlooked.

For instance, he broke a story about depleted uranium that made its way to the halls of Congress and was attached to a bill.

Shortly after the newspaper published a cover story about the exportation of jobs and difficulties businesses have had in dealing with Export-Import Bank of America, its chairman and president resigned.

The newspaper published a blistering editorial about voter inconsistencies pertaining to the 2004 presidential election entitled, "Ohio – Ground Zero."

Government workers with "inside information" began contacting the newspaper, wanting investigations of their agencies.

Smith increased opinion/editorial content of the newspaper to include a vast array of writers whom he had studied and whose work he appreciated.

And finally, he opted to regularly feature someone or something iconoclastic on the paper's cover, which has become the standard format for *The Iconoclast*.

The Lone Star Iconoclast
reporting team

W. Leon Smith
Publisher

Nathan Diebnow
Associate Editor/Columnist

Deborah Mathews
Reporter/Photographer

Gene Ellis Sills, Ed.D.
Reporter/Columnist

Michael Harvey
Publisher's Assistant

EPILOGUE

By W. Leon Smith

The news media draws a lot of criticism, often deservedly so. But life for the reporter in the field is often not easy.

When events unfold, such as those in Crawford during the twenty-six days of the vigil, much attention is given to the organizers and participants, what they go through, their message, and how they survive day to day.

Reporters lug around heavy equipment, walk the tar-melted streets, often in advance of the parade, put up with the same weather, and are frequently berated.

They are criticized if they stay and are criticized worse if they go.

Reporters must stay alert during these activities, so as not to miss something important. Their job depends on it. They are stressed. They must be creative, while at the same time collecting facts. They must remain even-tempered, and unemotional under trying and upsetting conditions.

When the participants of the activities are finally exhausted and are ready to call it quits to recuperate, members of the press who have endured just as much abuse if not more, must file their stories, process photographs, hit tight deadlines, and quite often put in several more hours of difficult work.

The days are very long and tiring and the pressures are immense.

Our reporters would return to the office sunburned, hungry after missing lunch, worn out, ready to drop, knowing that there were hours of intense work left to do. Reporters for other communications companies were in the same boat.

This situation occurs not only at events such as those in Crawford, but is an every-day exercise. It takes time, money, and enormous energy to put in the long hours, endure less-than-favorable conditions, and deal with individuals who are quick to be uncooperative when reporters are covering stories or events.

Many people are of the mindset that reporters deserve abuse. Our take is that most of the reporters in the Sheehan barnyard were treated with respect.

Walt Disney once said, "My only hope is that we never lose sight of one thing, that it was all started by a mouse."

In Cindy Sheehan's case, it all started with her determination to meet with President Bush, and that remained the root focus of the twenty-six days in Crawford.

It was this determination of spirit that not only created a leader, but also gave rise to throngs of followers with similar issues to voice. The target from both hemispheres of argument was the war in Iraq.

Sheehan said she wanted the war to again inhabit the front pages of the nation's newspapers. She wanted news broadcasts to re-evaluate what the top stories should be. She wanted answers cleansed in truth.

President Bush did not meet with her.

But because of her resolve to stave off fire-ants and the blistering Texas heat while camped in a ditch awaiting his attention, she captured the imagination of America. She caused public debate over the war. Stalwarts of both sides awakened from a grueling apathy tinged in silence.

For twenty-six days, before Hurricane Katrina obliterated New Orleans and Hurricane Rita pounded Texas with a resounding encore, people throughout America were thinking about dead soldiers and mothers and the human costs of war. And now, the hurricanes had added unbridled poverty to the list.

But in Crawford, Texas, Cindy Sheehan had given birth

to this century's first truly viable anti-war movement that would soon evolve into a 100,000 demonstrator march on Washington, D.C.

During these days our country became filled with Iconoclasts.

About the **disinformation**® [ALL ACCESS] series

ALL ACCESS is a new series of small, rapid response books addressing important social and political issues. While it usually takes months or years from the time an author writes a book to the time it appears on the shelves of libraries and book shops, **ALL ACCESS** provides authors an opportunity to see their writing on time-sensitive issues progress from ideas to actual books on sale in just weeks. The authors address important and often complex concepts in a detailed but plain spoken and easy-to-digest format.